Prentice-Hall

America's Role in World Affairs Series

Dankwart A. Rustow, Editor

RUPERT EMERSON
Africa and United States Policy

WALTER GOLDSTEIN
Military Strategy in World Politics

WILLIAM E. GRIFFITH
Cold War and Coexistence: Russia, China, and the United States

ERNST B. HAAS
The Web of Interdependence: The United States
and International Organizations

STANLEY HOFFMANN
Europe and United States Policy

CHARLES BURTON MARSHALL
The Burden of Decision: American Foreign Policy Since 1945

JOHN D. MONTGOMERY
Foreign Aid in International Politics

WILLIAM C. OLSON
The Making of United States Foreign Policy

DANKWART A. RUSTOW
The New Setting of World Politics

KALMAN H. SILVERT
Latin America and United States Policy

WAYNE A. WILCOX
Asia and United States Policy

RUPERT EMERSON
Harvard University

Africa
and
United States
Policy

PRENTICE-HALL, INC., ENGLEWOOD CLIFFS, N. J.

C

Library of Congress Catalog Card No.: 67-13354

Current Printing (last number):
10 9 8 7 6 5 4 3 2 1

Written under the auspices of
The Center for International Affairs
Harvard University

PRENTICE-HALL INTERNATIONAL, INC. *London*
PRENTICE-HALL OF AUSTRALIA, PTY. LTD. *Sydney*
PRENTICE-HALL OF CANADA, LTD. *Toronto*
PRENTICE-HALL OF INDIA (PRIVATE) LTD. *New Delhi*
PRENTICE-HALL OF JAPAN, INC. *Tokyo*

America's Role in World Affairs Series

Yood

Specialized knowledge and practical experience combine to lay the solid foundations for this survey of AMERICA'S ROLE IN WORLD AFFAIRS. Eleven distinguished authors distill their insights, refined in years spent as responsible government officials, as high-level advisers to governments, in prolonged field research, and in teaching at our leading universities. Their volumes emphasize the lasting realities underlying current conflict, the political forces in the present that will shape the world of the future. Separately, each volume in the series is a concise, authoritative analysis of a problem area of major significance. Taken as a whole, the series gives a broader and more diversified coverage than would be possible in a single book on American foreign policy and international relations.

An introductory volume by the series editor appraises the rapidly changing environment of foreign policy in the second half of the twentieth century—the revolution of modernization, the multiplication of sovereign states, and the tightening network of communication around the globe. In bold and deft strokes, William C. Olson analyzes the forces of public opinion, congressional action, and planning and implementation in the executive branch that combine to shape American foreign policy. Charles Burton Marshall takes the reader to the inner councils of United States policy as he retraces with wit, urbanity, and a lively sense of drama some of the crucial turning points in our foreign relations.

Three volumes deal systematically with some of the major instruments of contemporary foreign policy. Walter Goldstein cogently links the breathless pace of military technology in a nuclear age to some of the perennial dimensions of human conflict and strategic calculation. The wide range of uses—the possibilities and limitations—of foreign aid yield to John D. Montgomery's penetrating treatment. Ernst B. Haas combines sober realism with a passionate sense of human interdependence in his succinct account of the contemporary pattern of international organization.

Another group of volumes takes us to regions where the drama of modern international politics is being enacted. The intimate and yet often frustrating relations between the United States and Western Europe are sharply illuminated by Stanley Hoffmann's irony and subtle understanding. William E. Griffith clarifies the awesome issues of Cold War and coexistence in the triangular relations among the United States, the Soviet Union, and Communist China. Wayne A. Wilcox, in a synthesis of rare breadth and depth, allows the reader to grasp the full complexities of that geographic concept called Asia. The problems of new states, with their bitter memories of the colonial past and their ardent hopes for a better future, are presented with sympathy and skepticism in Rupert Emerson's volume on Africa. Kalman H. Silvert draws on two decades of travel and study and on his keen sense for the explosive issues of evolution vs. revolution as he sums up the record of our relations with Latin America.

The contributors have sought no consensus of policy preference and no narrow uniformity of scholarly method. They share a conviction that policy must operate within a context of circumstance that allows now a wider, now a narrower, choice of alternatives and that sound policy must be formulated from a thorough knowledge of that context. They hold that valid theory in the social sciences must rise upon solid empirical foundations. They also believe that clarity and conciseness do not detract from true scholarship but, on the contrary, enhance it. Within such broad assumptions, each author has applied his specialized knowledge and his practical experience to one distinctive facet of AMERICA'S ROLE IN WORLD AFFAIRS.

DANKWART A. RUSTOW

Preface

To seek to confine an Africa in ferment between the two static covers of a book is in many ways an exercise in futility. The mere multiplicity of African countries renders it impossible to do justice to all of them and to the relations of the United States with them. When the United Nations got under way in 1945, the entire African continent was represented in it by only four states, but two decades later the African membership had soared tenfold to 39, of which 34 states, including Ethiopia and the Sudan, were located south of the Sahara. Nor is the matter one of numbers only, for these African countries differ greatly among themselves, and each is caught up in a revolutionary process of change whose course and destination remain in large measure obscure. What is said about this or that country today may need to be drastically revised by tomorrow. Eternal verities, concealed beneath the surface of the often tumultuous sequence of events, are more likely to be revealed to succeeding generations than to ours.

This book has as its essential purpose an examination of the relations between the United States and Africa, relations which have taken on almost totally new dimensions in the last decade as colonialism was swept into history's wastebasket. Particularly since the Gold Coast was transformed into independent Ghana in 1957, American interest in, and intercourse with, Africa has increased immensely, and yet it remains one of the complicating factors that on the whole Africa continues to be of only peripheral concern to the United States. No effort to render simple and unambiguous the relations between America and Americans on one side and Africa and Africans on the other can hope for success, because these relations are in fact highly complex, diverse, and even contradictory within themselves.

In the limited space allotted to this volume it has seemed desirable to concentrate on the relations of governments rather than of peoples, even though the loss involved in such a decision is by no means inconsiderable. As a result, the private, nongovernmental activities of American foundations, churches, corporations, trade unions, and many other groups have been unduly slighted.* Most notably inadequate attention is given to the fascinating but intricate and amorphous problem of the many types of relationships between Negro Americans and Africans on both sides of the ocean.

A further limitation is that North Africa has been almost totally excluded from consideration. There is no occasion to reopen here the old and continuing controversy as to whether Africa north and south of the Sahara is, and should be dealt with as, a single entity or two separable realms. Either side of this argument can be effectively supported, and the answer depends in good part on the particular purpose to be served in the inquiry which is being conducted. For the present purpose it did not appear that much of significance was lost by introducing North Africa only where its affairs had inescapable relevance to those of sub-Saharan Africa, and much was gained by reducing the number of states to be surveyed. The reader is hereby warned that in order to avoid constant repetition of "Africa south of the Sahara" or "sub-Saharan Africa" or "Black Africa," I have throughout used the word "Africa" with reference only to the countries south of the Sahara. Where North Africa is included, I have used some such phrase as "Africa as a whole" or "the entire continent." In similar fashion I have referred to the former Belgian Congo, now Congo-Kinshasa, formerly Congo-Leopoldville, as the Congo; where the former French Congo, Congo-Brazzaville, is brought in, it is so identified.

The aid which I have received from many sources, including the invaluable contributions of students, would turn into an intolerably long list if I were to seek to name all those on whom I have drawn. I am in debt to all of them. In particular, I should like to express my gratitude to James S. Coleman, former Director of the African Studies Center, and Richard P. Longaker, Chairman of the Department of Political Science, both of the University of California, Los Angeles, for enabling me to spend a term at UCLA, in the course of which much of this book was written. To the staff of the African Studies Center I should like to give thanks for warm hospitality and much concrete assistance. The Center for International Affairs at Harvard has also made it possible for me to carry on the research and writing necessary for the completion of this volume. My associates in the Center have been generous in the aid and guidance they have afforded me. Miss Margot Metzger has stood by to assist in polishing and checking and has cheerfully borne the load of typing which was involved.

RUPERT EMERSON

---

* A useful survey of nongovernmental American involvements in Africa—educational, foundations, religious, business, etc.—is contained in *African Programs of U.S. Organizations,* compiled by Jacqueline S. Mithun, Department of State Publication 7902 (Washington: Govt. Printing Office, 1965).

Contents

1

The United States and Africa

On November 24, 1964, American planes carried Belgian paratroopers to Stanleyville in the Congo. Washington and Brussels proclaimed it a mission of mercy intended to rescue hostages from the rebel Congolese forces, but many leading Africans denounced it as an intolerable return to imperialist aggression.

No other event has comparably tested the entire fabric of American relations with Africa. It might be seen as marking the end of a honeymoon that had already experienced some stormy passages, or as the last phase of disillusionment in the vanishing of an age of innocence shared by both Africans and Americans. In the immediate aftermath in the Security Council, Adlai Stevenson characterized it as "a gallant and successful effort to save human lives of many nationalities and colors," while a number of speakers damned it in unmeasured terms as a "wanton and deliberate massacre of Congolese people," as genocide "to exterminate the black inhabitants," and as being linked to the murders of Patrice Lumumba and John F. Kennedy and the death of Dag Hammarskjold—or must that be taken as murder, too? America's standing in much of Africa had already been seriously prejudiced by the backing that the United States had given to Moise Tshombe since he took over as Premier in Leopoldville in July, 1964. Air and other support for the Congolese forces, spearheaded by white mercenaries largely recruited in South Africa and neighboring countries, and under-the-counter provision of American civilian "technicians" and Cuban refugees who flew planes to support military operations had proved more than many Africans could stomach; but it was the paratroop drop that set off the all-out assault upon the United States.

As Africans saw it, the United States had demonstrated that it was irresponsible in the use of its vast power. While negotiations initiated by the Organization of African Unity (OAU) were still in progress, the United States joined with Belgium, with the backing of Britain, to undertake a military venture in the heart of Africa, timed to coincide with the arrival at the gates of Stanleyville of the detested mercenary forces of Tshombe, who was seen as a traitor to the African cause. Africans scornfully repudiated the rescue operation as no more than a cover for a military operation designed to ensure that Stanleyville fell to Tshombe. The sufferings and slaughter of Africans were held to be of no concern to the United States and the European colonialists, whereas danger to the life of a white man justified military intervention in an African state. The disgust and fear roused among Africans by the Stanleyville affair were felt to be confirmed when, soon afterward, the United States expanded its military operations in Vietnam, including the bombing of North Vietnam, and when American forces moved into the Dominican Republic in the spring of 1965. The spectre of neo-colonialism took on flesh and blood.

But not all Africans shared, or at least openly acknowledged, the bitter sentiments expressed in the United Nations and elsewhere—and their feelings were also woven into the fabric of African-American relations. Most notably Nigeria and a number of the formerly French states took Stanleyville calmly or even endorsed the Belgian-American action, and soon the organization that embraced most of the French-speaking countries was prepared to accept Tshombe's Congo as a member. It is, of course, also true that in Nigeria and other acquiescent states, liberal and left elements joined in the denunciation of the military intervention. Not all Africans denounced the United States, nor was it reasonable to suppose that the grievance would everywhere be very long remembered in a world so swiftly changing, but enough had joined in the denunciation to force a sober reappraisal of the nature of the relationships between African countries and the United States. It must also not be left out of the reckoning that for many Americans, the entire Congo experience and the murder of hostages in particular had a drastic effect in rearousing the image of Africans as a savage and primitive people. A return to amicable and cooperative arrangements was far from being excluded for the future, but that future would necessarily have a different tone and quality.

The honeymoon, the age of innocence—insofar as they actually existed and were not merely an illusion of an extraordinary period—derived from circumstances and relationships that were unique.

On the African side, the distinctive event was the achievement within the span of a few years of independence which, a decade earlier, almost no one would have assumed could come so soon. Indeed, it might be argued that the amazing sweep of decolonization in Africa was a by-product of the liberation of major Asian colonies rather than something that happened according to a timetable particularly oriented to African conditions. In Asia, mature and well-established national movements such as those in India, Indonesia, and the Philippines—and Japan's overthrow and discrediting of European colonialism in Southeast Asia—established with a logic of their own that independence could not be long delayed.

It was in the climate of anticolonialism, spreading from Asia to the rest of the world and ably urged on its way by the Communists, that African nationalism sprouted into luxuriant growth. Most African anticolonial or nationalist movements had only very tenuous roots, if any, before World War II. Foreshadowings of nationalism can perhaps be found everywhere in bits and pieces of movements, often concealed within a religious guise. On the West Coast, among a few authentic early samples are the Aborigenes Rights Protection Society in the Gold Coast or the West African National Congress, but it was only in the postwar period that unmistakable and large-scale movements began to spread over the continent. The African political leaders were presumably almost as much surprised as anybody else at the speed with which their countries gained independence. In the French colonial territories, in particular, although political parties and political activity flourished in the postwar atmosphere, the demand for independence was not effectively put forward until the mid-1950's. The Belgian Congo knew overt and organized political movements of any kind only in the two or three years immediately preceding independence in 1960.

As far as the two major colonial powers, Britain and France, were concerned, it was, for all practical purposes, not until after the war that the first significant moves were made toward an extension of self-government. Both were obviously weakened by the losses which two world wars had inflicted on them, but it is also clear that they, like the rest of the world, were affected by the anticolonial spirit which found increasing expression in the UN. In the first years after the war, independence for their African dependencies seemed far away, but they were well aware of the need for colonial reform and for getting started on processes of development previously pursued in only an intermittent and negligent fashion. Characteristically, their responses to the new challenge of the postwar period diverged sharply. In terms of moves that might have independence as their outcome, if not deliberately their goal, the British far outstripped the French by introducing increasing installments of self-government while the French set as their ultimate target the equal integration of their territories into a single greater France, giving African leaders a role in the governing institutions in Paris. With the experience of Indochina behind them and the bitter war still raging in Algeria, de Gaulle's government at the end of the 1950's reversed the course of French policy by tranquilly accepting the independence of its African domains, thus bringing a baker's dozen of new states into the UN in the single amazing year of 1960, which also saw the entry of Nigeria, by far the most populous African state, and of the embattled Congo.

What stands out is that, with rare exceptions, the African states departed from their colonial overlords in reasonably amicable agreement on the timing and circumstances of independence. The degree of good will and agreement of course varied significantly from country to country, and it would be a misleading picture to see it as composed wholly of sweetness and light. The Algerian conflict spread its shadows southward; Guinea departed with bitterness on both sides; Nkrumah was taken from jail in 1951 to lead the Gold Coast to self-government; the Mau Mau uprising and its suppression ravaged Kenya for years; rebellion in Madagascar shortly after the war was suppressed with much bloodshed; the Federation of Rhodesia and Nyasaland met with increasing resistance from the Africans within it, and open conflict broke out in Nyasaland in 1959. These and many similar episodes demonstrate that even without taking into account continued Portuguese colonialism and white rule in Southern Rhodesia, Africa's accession to independence was not a simple matter of Africans seeking, and the colonial powers granting, freedom; and yet it was largely a surprisingly peaceful transition carried through with exemplary toleration on both sides.

Nowhere would it be possible to say that the British or the French put up anything approaching a last-ditch resistance; indeed the more striking feature is the erosion of the will to power. It would be difficult to find any territory where the pressure became so intense as virtually to enforce withdrawal, although in a number of areas the ability of the colonial authorities to make their control effective was severely challenged. The situation seems rather to have been a more complex combination of forces. One element was undoubtedly the rise of African nationalism; but another element was the British, French, and Belgian reading of the handwriting on the wall which spelled the end of colonialism. The willingness to pay the price of repression had largely vanished, and in a few instances, as in some of the French territories, independence was granted in response to no discernible pressure of significance. If part of the calculation was that more could be salvaged for the future in this fashion than by attempting to hold on to everything, this was surely a calculation which the prudent man would make. Nor was it necessarily against the interests of the African peoples themselves thus to maintain amicable and even intimate relations with the former colonial powers, even though it promptly opened the door to charges of neo-colonialism. It is as understandable that the Africans should stress the heroic nature of their struggle against colonial powers as that the Europeans should exaggerate their voluntary generosity in accepting African independence.

This state of affairs made friendly intercourse between the United States and emerging African countries far easier than it might have been otherwise. African leaders ordinarily came to power in their own countries with no deep and immediate sense of grievance, however vehemently they repudiated colonialism as an institution, and they continued to utilize the services of a large number of expatriate officials and experts during an extended interim period. The fact that the United States was intimately allied with the former colonial power was therefore not a matter to which any great attention needed to be paid, even though the universal drift was toward some version of neutralism. The American image was enhanced by its traditional aura of anticolonialism, and John F. Kennedy sought to link the American revolutionary heritage to the revolutions sweeping Asia and Africa. Since the winning of independence had not been an issue bitterly fought over and requiring third parties to take a public stand, the United States could be credited with a backing for the anticolonial cause which it had not been necessary to demonstrate.

In view of its hesitant approach to self-determination, the United States may have received more credit than it deserved, even though the colonial powers no doubt felt that America was an untrustworthy ally where dependencies were concerned. In an important speech on the colonial problem, Assistant Secretary of State Henry A. Byroade in 1953 endorsed "eventual self-determination for all peoples" and expressed his belief that "evolutionary development to this end should move forward with minimum delay." [1] In the same breath, he pointed to what he termed the hard, inescapable fact that "premature independence can be dangerous, retrogressive and destructive," praised much of the work of the colonial powers in Africa including the Portuguese, and called for frank recognition that American security was linked to the strength and stability of these powers and their legitimate interests in their dependencies.

Yet it is also evident that the United States welcomed the African countries' transition to independence and that it was prepared speedily to adapt itself to the new situation even though, out of deference to France, it hesitated unduly in recognizing Guinea. Having previously paid only minimal attention to African problems, the United States almost overnight created an elaborate network of relationships with Africa. To mention here only a single phase of these relationships, the rebirth of Black Africa, usually dated from Ghana's independence in 1957, came at a time when the United States was deeply committed to the principle of foreign aid, and prompt moves were made to bring the newly independent African states within the framework of the aid program.

Whatever the disappointments or suspicions of the Africans or what they saw as the shortcomings of the United States, it was on the whole true that as African independence began to unfold, not only the American and African governments but also the peoples as well, regarded each other with good will and undue optimism as to the future. Since the Africans felt no need at the outset to damn the United States as an imperialist oppressor, they could assume that America would be sympathetic to their needs and desires, be a source of material bounty and technical assistance, and open up another door to the great outside world than that provided by the colonial powers. The American outlook tended to be equally optimistic as far as the African states were concerned: here was an array of new countries with whom friendly relations had been promptly established, whose development should be promoted both for their own sake and to aid them in evading the dangerous wiles

[1] United States Department of State Press Release, No. 605, October 30, 1953. Vernon McKay has characterized this speech as "the classic masterpiece of American ambiguity on the colonial question." (*Africa in World Politics*. New York: Harper, 1963, p. 320.)

of communism, and whose policies might be expected to be in general accord with those of the United States. On the American side, special pressures were exercised by the sense of guilt deriving from the slave trade, slavery, and discrimination, and important elements among the 20 million Negro Americans were stirred by the emergence into full daylight of the continent to which they traced their origins.

The prevailing views were optimistically friendly, even though on both sides many were skeptical or hostile, as in the African abhorrence of the color bar in the United States. One essential cause for optimism was that both for the African countries and the United States, relationships and policies were being written afresh on what came surprisingly close to being a clean slate. Both sides were inclined to be on their best behavior at the outset of this new relationship. At least, no clash of interest was yet visible, and at best, it seemed plausible to look to collaboration for common purposes.

As far as the African states were concerned, they were by definition newborn, and could have no established foreign policy save as it was inherited from the colonial regime or had been laid out in advance by the nationalist parties. On the American side, although relations with the African continent reached far back and took many forms, the continuing ties in the present century were so slight and inconsequential that it was both possible and necessary to make virtually a new beginning in the era of African independence starting in the mid-1950's. As the African states had to create foreign policy from the ground up, so the United States was also in a position to start afresh in shaping its African policies with a mimimum of commitments and established doctrines but subject, of course, to its relations with its allies and the contingencies of the Cold War.

The American ability to shape policy toward Africa without undue constraints was enhanced by the fact that Africa was an even less known continent to the Russians and Chinese, and their access to it was much more limited and difficult. However much Africa might be held susceptible to future Communist penetration, the Communists had achieved almost no hold when independence was getting under way. Many members of the small African elite which was coming into power had, of course, some exposure to Marxist thinking and organizational techniques, but only a few had been sufficiently indoctrinated to look primarily to Moscow or Peking or to assume that because the United States was capitalistic it necessarily constituted an active menace.

Another good omen was that the United States by the end of the 1950's had left behind it the pactomania that led it to consolidate its anti-Communist front by signing up as many states as possible in mutual security treaties, such as SEATO and CENTO, modeled at least in principle on NATO. Such a policy could have had only the effect of dividing the African states and infuriating all those who looked to African unity and to nonalignment. Washington had come around to the sensible view that neutralism was not necessarily a confession of sin but was often well adapted to the needs and circumstances of the new countries. In fact, African neutralism tended to be shaded toward friendship with the West, which made American anti-Communist pressure generally unnecessary and all the more resented when American spokesmen could not restrain their impulse to indulge in it. One of the merits of independence was the ability, denied under colonialism, to have direct contact with the other peoples of the world, and among these peoples the Communist powers not only loomed large, but were made even more interesting by the reiterated American denunciation of them. As the African leaders saw it, not communism but colonialism was the enemy, followed by the need to make war on poverty, ignorance, and disease. If many Americans found it difficult to accept this evaluation, at least the absence of a direct and overt Communist threat in Africa made the establishment of congenial relations with Africans easier than it might have been otherwise. As promptly as possible, however, the Russians and Chinese followed the Americans in moving into Africa, bringing this phase of the age of innocence to an end.

In summary, the identifiable interests of both the United States and the African countries in the early years of African independence were rather loosely defined and appeared not to be in conflict with each other. Vice-President Nixon, on his return from Ghana's independence ceremonies in March, 1957, could report to the President, "There is no area in the world today in which the prestige of the United States is more uniformly high" than in the African countries which he visited.[2]

In the decade following Ghana's independence, that prestige has undergone a succession of dramatic ups and downs, and official American interest in Africa has also fluctuated markedly. As the number of African states multiplied and their policies as well as those of the United States came to be more sharply defined, it was inevitable that tensions and conflicts should arise. The romantic illusion both of African unity and of a common purpose linking the United States and African countries was bound to be challenged by the hard facts of divergent national interests. The independence of almost all African colonies has brought with it an immense increase and diversification of American relations with Africa, but the task of accomplishing even a minimum of what remains to be done has barely been started. The potential centers of trouble are legion, but nowhere is the threat as grave as in the vast southern end of the continent which clings to white domination.

[2] Richard Nixon, *The Emergence of Africa, Report to the President by Vice-President Nixon on His Trip to Africa* (Washington: Department of State, April, 1957). In this report the Vice-President presumably overestimated the existing Communist threat: "Africa is a priority target for the international communist movement. I gathered the distinct impression that the communist leaders consider Africa today to be as important in their designs for world conquest as they considered China to be twenty-five years ago."

2

What Is Africa?

What is this Africa with which the United States has come to be belatedly and intimately entangled?

Occupying many volumes, an adequate answer would produce no single picture of Africa but rather an overwhelming sense of vastness and diversity. One of the outstanding pioneer American Africanists, Melville J. Herskovits, commented that there are "as many Africas as there are questions touching on the peoples of the geographical entity we call Africa, their historical past, and their future." [1]

As a purely physical entity, Africa is a single immense continent, but if any criteria other than sheer land mass are called upon, it is neither as separable from the rest of the world nor as united within itself as the map may suggest. Egypt links it with the Arab world, and the Nile rises far south in the heart of Africa. The surrounding seas have been used as channels of intercourse with other continents and peoples, and the Sahara Desert has served as both a barrier and a sea to be crossed. Islam has swept across the desert deep into sub-Saharan Africa; the Europeans coming by sea have for centuries been established in South Africa; for many more centuries, East Africa and Asia have been in touch with each other across the Indian Ocean; and the Arab dhows have voyaged down the East Coast. The natural divisions of geography have conspired with, and have been superseded by, the divisions of religion, language, race,

[1] *Symposium on Africa* (Wellesley, Mass.: Wellesley College, 1960), p. 19.

and ethnic group. Most recently, colonialism imposed a still newer set of barriers and divisions which have with very rare exceptions served to demarcate the states forming the political map of Africa. Common subjection to European colonial rule and the common rising against it have also helped to lay foundations for an all-embracing pan-African unity, first glimpsed from across the Atlantic by descendants of African slaves.

The precolonial history of Africa is currently in a peculiarly active state of re-examination, challenging the belief, so consoling to those who would either promote the slave trade or impose colonial rule, that since Africans are primitive and barbarous, they have no history comparable to that of other "historic peoples." White supremacy found expression in looking down on the black as racially inferior, indeed, as barely human. In the new Africa, black is a color to be proud of, and *Négritude,* the essence of being a Negro, is pride in belonging to a great segment of mankind which has made its own distinctive contribution. The historians have had a field day in demonstrating that even though much of Africa's past is lost through the lack of written languages and more permanent architectural structures, the record demonstrates many points of high achievement. Archeological discoveries, the search for untapped written sources, the exploitation of the riches of oral history, and other devices and techniques have revealed a past which had been largely lost from sight.

Despite the burst of contemporary discovery, much of the African past and present remains obscure. Nothing approaching a certain answer can be given to vital, present-day questions; for example: how many people live in Africa and how many languages do they speak?

For the entire continent it appears that a figure of 280 million may be set as an educated guess of the total population, but any such figure rests upon shaky local estimates and enumerations. Ethiopia's official estimate of 22 million people is a suspiciously round figure, and Nigeria's two censuses of 1962–1963 ended up with a total figure of over 55 million, which many regarded as being unconscionably inflated for political reasons.

Of the 280 million people attributed to Africa as a whole, some 60 million live in the five North African countries on the Mediterranean. In South Africa are another 18 million, of whom some 3.5 million are white and nearly 550,000 Asian. For other sub-Saharan territories where substantial numbers of Europeans have settled, estimates of the white populations at their highest were roughly as follows: Rhodesia 220,000, Kenya 60,000, Angola 200,000 or more, and Mozambique 65,000. Of these territories only Kenya has come to independence and African rule; in the others the government remains in white hands.

As far as the number of languages is concerned, the situation is markedly worse than it is in relation to people, since a number of disputes still rage over identification and interrelationship of African languages and dialects. The extent of the difficulty is apparent in this comment of an experienced student of African languages: "Africa is a very big continent with a large, widely dispersed population speaking between one and two thousand different languages—most of them *very* different." [2]

Of these languages only a few—such as Swahili, Hausa, Amharic, Ibo, Yoruba, and Somali—are spoken by more than a million people, and none embraces as many as twenty million, while very limited communities use the great bulk "between one and two thousand." Only in the rarest of cases does any one of the present multiplicity of states in Africa possess a single national language spoken by the mass of its population. The standard pattern is that each of the states contains a number of indigenous languages, while either English or French, introduced as the lingua franca under colonial rule, was established as the national, or at least as the official language after independence, despite the inability of most of the people to make use of so alien a tongue.

Socially and politically the African continent has been highly fragmented in terms of its indigenous linguistic and ethnic communities. Despite occasional heated charges by nationalists of the pan-African persuasion that Western imperialism had shattered African unity—Balkanization is the standard term of abuse—it is obvious that no unity existed prior to the colonial take-over. The political entities created by the imperial powers were actually substantially larger—in many instances very much larger—than the pre-existing tribal entities or the empires created by the Africans themselves. What the Europeans did was to bring into being a number of new political units that lumped together or cut across the older ethnic groupings in an often erratic and arbitrary fashion. In a sense, the net effect was to compound the confusion of Africa's fragmentation, since many new sets of frontiers, and hence of potential future loyalties, were superimposed on the tribal and other communities, joining them together under a single colonial rule or, not infrequently, dividing a tribe between two or more colonies.

In carving up the African continent, the colonial powers created the states, and prospectively the nations, now constituting the African political community. Since they had no prior existence, one must look to the effects of colonialism in the first instance for such inner coherence as each of these states possesses; but the effective reign of colonialism in Africa was brief. For almost all the African territories, the colonial regimes had no significant impact until the last years of the nineteenth century or substantially later for much of the hinterland. Even where coastal contact between Europeans and Africans had a centuries-old history, as in carrying on the slave trade, virtually no penetration in depth took place until the time of the Berlin Conference of 1884-1885 or later. Even when colonial rule was established, some time inevitably was lost before European control made itself felt throughout the entire territory included within the newly demarcated colonial boundaries. The back country saw far less of the European presence than the urban centers, the mines, or plantations, and different regions of the same

[2] Robert G. Armstrong, "Vernacular Languages and Cultures in Modern Africa," in *Language in Africa*, ed. John Spencer (Cambridge: Cambridge University, 1963), p. 65. See also Joseph Greenberg, *The Languages of Africa* (Bloomington: Indiana University, 1963).

colony were sometimes accorded very different treatment, most strikingly illustrated perhaps in the distinctive system adopted for Northern Nigeria, compared to the two southern regions. Colonialism gave Africans both limited and diverse exposure to the kind of world in which they were going to have to live.

Whether their work was done well or badly, the imperial powers made the basic contribution of shaping the sovereign states that now speak for Africa at home and abroad. In a perverse fashion it might also be said that they made the further great contribution of furnishing the target at which the nationalist movements directed their fire. Each nationalist movement, even though it may also have drawn on the ideas and slogans of pan-Africanism, concentrated its attack upon the colonial regime in its own country, and its success was marked by taking over the governmental machinery which had served the colonial masters.

The independent states of Africa differ from each other in many significant respects; and despite the hopes of pan-African unity, the differences tend to grow greater as each country pursues its separate destiny in its own fashion. There are, however, certain broad lines of common identity running through all of Black Africa, such as its poverty, its widespread illiteracy and educational inadequacies, and the problems and nature of its political systems.

The fundamental proposition must be that Africa is peopled by poor countries which have made only a tentative start toward achieving for themselves the potentialities of power and well-being that the advanced countries have reached. Distinctions can, of course, be drawn between African countries in terms both of the standard of living of their people and of the progress they have made in development—the Ivory Coast is substantially better off than Mali, and Kenya has a more highly developed agriculture and industry than Tanzania—but differences between African countries on such scores are far smaller than the vast gap dividing them all from advanced peoples. Only the white communities of South Africa and Rhodesia can be ranked with the advanced sectors of the world in terms of their standards of living and highly developed economies. Some of the basic facts and figures were laid out by Assistant Secretary of State Williams in a speech on March 18, 1965:

> The average per capita income for the continent as a whole is about $120 a year and as low as $40 a year in some parts of the continent. This is the lowest per capita income of any geographic region in the world—almost twice as low as the next lowest region—and there is little local capital for economic development. . . .
>
> Although Africa is primarily an agricultural continent and 75 per cent of the people make their living from the land, the average African farmer is only about 4 per cent as productive as his counterpart in North America.
>
> Education presents much the same picture. While there is a cultural and sophisticated elite, about 85 per cent of Africa's people are illiterate. There is a crucial lack of trained people. . . .
>
> Communications are extremely poor throughout much of Africa. . . . Health is another major problem. Every known tropical disease exists in the continent, taking the lives of one of every five African children.

There is a severe shortage of doctors, nurses, and other health personnel. Where we have one doctor for every 740 people, the ratio for Africa (excluding South Africa) is one for every 22,500 people.[3]

The drive for modernization and development is under way everywhere, but the pace of advance is slow and hesitant; and in Africa as elsewhere, even where development is being vigorously pressed, the advanced world is striding ahead more rapidly than the underdeveloped countries are catching up.

Hampered by local lack of private capital or skilled and venturesome entrepreneurs, those who seek development are faced by two polar opposites of policy, although in actuality every state operates on the basis of some mixture of the two. One policy opens the doors wide to foreign enterprise and investment. This is the policy which Houphouet-Boigny has adopted in the Ivory Coast, but it is not generally attractive to nationalists just out from under alien rule and fearful of falling victim to neo-colonialism. The other policy involves assigning to the state a predominant role in promoting development, a role which the African elites generally find congenial because of the favor in which African Socialism is held. Capitalism is identified with alien imperialism, while African Socialism, however loosely defined, represents the realization of a cherished tradition of communal collaboration, free of all exploitation. Any version of socialism, however, requires a coherent governmental structure and a reasonably efficient and impartial administration, which is more than most African states can now be said to possess. Despite the devoted and capable service of many African political leaders and administrators, it is evident that the multiplication of low-level bureaucracy, favoritism, corruption, and sheer inefficiency render local efforts and foreign aid far less effective than they might otherwise be. Kwame Nkrumah found capitalism "too complicated a system for a newly independent nation," [4] but socialism surely makes even greater demands.

Heroic strides have been made in most African countries to meet the demand for an expansion of education which will enable the rising generation to take its place in the modern world. The costs are, however, very great, the ability to supply qualified teachers in large numbers is limited, and the adjustment of the supply of school-leavers at various levels to the manpower needs of the country is always difficult. A standard bottleneck throughout Africa has been the very restricted secondary education available, denying advancement to many able primary school students and curtailing the ranks of those qualified for higher education.

[3] Department of State Press Release No. 48, p. 3. In a letter written to me on November 23, 1965 Andrew M. Kamarck of the World Bank presented the matter in the following dramatic terms: "The total gross national product of sub-Saharan Africa is estimated at about $30 billion for 1964. This is nominally about 5 per cent of the GNP of the United States and roughly equivalent to the GNP of, say, 10 million people in the Los Angeles metropolitan area. Furthermore, although the share of South Africa has been declining, about one-third of the total GNP of sub-Saharan Africa was produced in South Africa, which has less than one-tenth of the total African population."

[4] Kwame Nkrumah, *Ghana: The Autobiography of Kwame Nkrumah* (New York: Nelson, 1957), p. xvi.

Despite the drive toward development and the spread of education, a serious gap still divides the dominant governing elite, in varying degree familiar with the modern world, and the mass of the people, still illiterate and not far removed from the traditional society. Intermediate strata are increasingly coming into existence, but the gap remains of basic significance for an understanding of the dynamics of African society and politics. It represents not only the distinction between rulers and ruled, but also in many instances between the bare bones of a subsistence economy and the ability to command the good things of life. The palaces which some of Africa's leaders have built for themselves have become notorious, and the large Mercedes goes with bureaucratic or political success. René Dumont has calculated that it would take the average African peasant thirty-six years of hard labor to equal the salary of an African deputy for six months, which would in fact involve only a month and a half of work in the deputy's official capacity.[5]

The illiteracy and poverty of the mass are surely not unrelated to the overwhelming swing toward one-party government, replacing the expectations of a postcolonial constitutional democracy by the harsher reality of the use of democratic forms to achieve authoritarian control. In many instances it has been a single leader—a Nkrumah, Touré, Kenyatta, or Houphouet-Boigny—who appeared to dominate the scene, personifying the remote abstractions of state and government in flesh-and-blood reality to an unsophisticated and fragmented people.

The hold of the one-party system can be explained and justified on a number of grounds in addition to the universal desire of the "ins" to hold on to prestige and power. The most fundamental proposition, though not one which is always avowed, is presumably contained in Sukarno's term: guided democracy, which implies that the gap between elite and mass can be filled only by those on top taking the guidance in their own hands. A firm government of national unity is inescapable, it has been contended, if the war against poverty, disease, and ignorance is to be won and if the sacrifices which development calls for are to be successfully enforced. A more specifically African consideration is that in tribally divided countries where there is no tradition of a loyal opposition, a serious danger is the emergence of tribal parties whose separatist inclinations threaten national unity. Furthermore, African spokesmen have protested that a multi-party system reflects the division into classes of the capitalist world, whereas African society has no such class cleavage.

Until the epidemic of military coups broke out in 1965, the one-party system approached universality in Africa. The two most striking exceptions were the confusion of parties in the Congo and the three major parties of Nigeria, each with its own federally-anchored tribal-regional base. For the rest, it is arguable that to point out the universality of one-party systems does not establish very much because of the differences between the several systems in formal structure and political style. If the most distinctive is the unique pluralism introduced into Tanzania's ruling party by Nyerere, it is also true that, say, the Ivory Coast, Ghana, Mali,

[5] René Dumont, *L'Afrique Noire Est Mal Partie* (Paris: Editions du Seuil, 1962), p. 66.

Kenya, and Malawi all differed very substantially from each other, save in
the effort to deny by law or in fact that any rival party may challenge the
monopolistic hold of the party in power.

By far the most significant challenge to the ruling parties came with
the series of coups undertaken by the military in late 1965 and early
1966, when civilian regimes fell in the Congo, Nigeria, Ghana, Dahomey,
the Central African Republic, and Upper Volta. Although much still remains obscure about these military take-overs, it appears to be clear that
they represent a widespread disaffection with the failure of the civilian
regimes to make headway in development of all sorts and a widespread
disgust with political corruption and favoritism. That the military are
likely to be a force working for national unity in each country and that
they will attack the shortcomings and abuses of the regimes they have
overthrown is generally to be expected; but it remains to be demonstrated
that they have the ability, the skilled manpower, and the integrity both to
do the job which is needed and to resist the temptations which betrayed
some of their civilian predecessors. It has been evident in several instances
that a relatively tiny handful of armed men could overthrow a government; having overthrown it, can they replace it by something better?

Whether African rule is military or civilian or some mix of the two, it
will continue to be confronted by problems of adjustment and development which would tax the abilities of the most skilled and experienced
administrators and statesmen. Some part of the road has been covered,
but a long distance remains to be traveled, and a back-breaking load must
be carried in traversing it.

3

A Century of Afro-American Relations

For nearly a century following the Civil War, American governmental relations with Africa were slight and sporadic although missionary, economic, and other private contacts expanded. The official policies of the United States in relation to Africa rarely involved special consideration of the continent's particular circumstances, problems, and needs, and were far more likely to be reflections of general American positions. It was only when Africa began unmistakably to emerge from colonial overlordship in the mid-1950's that specifically African issues, demanding African answers, forced themselves on American attention. Even then Africa generally brought up the rear among the major areas of the world in terms of effective American interest. In relation to Africa, apart from Liberia, no special ties existed such as those which linked the United States to Europe, Latin America, or parts of Asia. The threatened carving up of China excited much interest in the United States, while the almost total colonial take-over of Africa aroused no American response, either of opposition or of participation in the scramble.

The guiding principles were isolation and noninvolvement, and Africa appeared to offer no adequate compensation for breaching them, nor were there any compelling circumstances to force concrete American stands and actions. Even the assumption of a standard American hostility to colonialism was not taken to have any present applicability to Africa south of the Sahara, which was no doubt seen as a dark continent of primitive peoples for whom colonial tutelage was in order.

As soon as such blanket statements concerning American noninvolvement in Africa have been made, it is, of course, necessary to qualify them in a number of particulars. An exception, for example, must always be made in the case of Liberia which the United States was never prepared to take over as a colony or even as a protectorate but which was nonetheless tucked somewhat erratically under the American wing. It is also necessary to single out the Negro community, or at least significant elements within it, as having a continuous and distinctive awareness of Africa, which the great bulk of Americans lacked. As a particular example, the Fascist overrunning of Ethiopia—the only old-established African state which had maintained its independence—had a poignant meaning for many Negro Americans which their white fellow citizens were unlikely to share.

Over the decades, the United States took part in several conferences dealing with African affairs, but succeeded in safeguarding itself from any lasting involvement. Thus it participated in the two conferences dealing with Morocco held in Madrid in 1880 and in Algeciras in 1906. In the Berlin Conference of 1884–1885, which gave its blessings to Leopold's Congo and laid down ground rules for the scramble for Africa, the United States played an active role, seeking assurances both of humanitarian treatment for the Africans and an open door for American commerce. President Cleveland, however, declined to submit the Final Act of this Conference to the Senate, and Secretary of State Bayard asserted that the United States was unprepared to accept political engagements "in so remote and undefined a region as that of the Congo Basin." [1]

In the Boer War of 1899 to 1902, the United States formally acted upon its traditional policy of neutrality and aloofness, but Secretary of State Hay made clear his attachment to Great Britain and his assumption that Britain could count on American friendship in the war despite much popular sympathy for the Boers. Impartial enforcement of American neutrality legislation, in fact, worked strongly in Britain's favor because of the wealth and maritime power which she commanded in contrast to the poor and land-bound Boer republics. It was typical of the American outlook of the time that virtually no one paid attention to the fate of the mass of the Africans who were given no other alternatives than subjection to Boer or Briton, depending on victory in the war.

The capture of the German colonies by Allied forces brought World War I to Africa, but the United States was not significantly drawn into African ventures or contacts as a result of the war. In the Versailles Peace Conference following the war, Africa figured in only a marginal capacity, of which the major feature was the division of the former German territories among Britain, France, Belgium, and South Africa under the new guise of the mandate system. As one of the principal architects of the peace settlement, Woodrow Wilson was involved in the creation of this first installment of international supervision in the colonial sphere; but despite his zeal for self-determination, he was not concerned to engage in any anticolonial crusade, nor did he indicate any special concern for

[1] See George Louis Beer, *African Questions at the Paris Peace Conference* (New York: Macmillan, 1923), p. 264, n. 16.

the specifically African features of the problem.[2] The United States declined to accept responsibility for any of the mandated territories; and by its failure to ratify the Versailles treaty and to join the League of Nations, it cut itself off from any direct connection with the management of the system. The American national interest in Africa was not found, in the succession to Woodrow Wilson, to reach much beyond pressure to maintain an open door, allowing American trade and economic interests access to the continent on a nondiscriminatory basis.

The two major American governmental involvements with Africa in the interwar decades were the continuing difficulties of Liberia and Mussolini's attack upon Ethiopia. In addition, there were, of course, many private contacts with Africa by groups and individuals, including such matters as the role of W.E.B. Du Bois in calling a series of Pan-African Congresses, starting in 1919 in Paris, and the spectacular, if fruitless, movement of Marcus Garvey, bearing the title of Provisional President of the African Republic, to secure the return of Negroes to Africa. Save in South Africa and Liberia, American trade and investment remained at a low ebb. As a forerunner of larger numbers later, a small flow of African students, some of them to achieve great distinction at home in the future, came to the United States.

Liberia's problems in the 1920's and 1930's centered about three often interrelated themes: the inability of the country to avoid the constant threat of financial disaster, the centrality of the Firestone interests, and the repeated accusation of the existence of widespread forced labor. The Liberian story has been too often told to need more than brief recapitulation here.[3] Established in the third decade of the last century as a refuge for both freed American slaves and Africans rescued from slave-trading ships, Liberia declared itself an independent republic in 1847 and was recognized by the United States in 1862. Harassed by boundary disputes with Britain and France and always plagued by the split between the dominant Americo-Liberians and the tribal Africans of the hinterland, Liberia had in many ways a checkered and unhappy history. In 1912 a loan of $1.7 million secured by the customs revenues was arranged, and provision was made for an American Receiver of Customs who was also Financial Adviser to the Liberian government. The first World War, however, totally disrupted Liberia's finances and expectations, but the United States Senate failed in 1922 to approve a credit of $5 million which was to be granted by Washington. Instead, in part under the pressure of the skyrocketing prices of Malayan and Indonesian rubber, the Firestone Company in 1926 secured a concession of 1 million acres and provided a credit of $5 million through a subsidiary. The administration of customs

[2] Lawrence E. Gelfand, *The Inquiry: American Preparations for the Peace, 1917-1919* (New Haven: Yale University, 1963) indicates the attention given to Africa in the materials prepared for the American delegation to the peace conference.

[3] See Raymond L. Buell, *The Native Problem in Africa* (New York: Macmillan, 1928), II, 704-890 and his *Liberia: A Century of Survival, 1847-1947* (Philadelphia: University of Pennsylvania, 1947); Raymond Bixler, *The Foreign Policy of the United States in Liberia* (New York: Pageant, 1957); and Nnamdi Azikiwe, *Liberia in World Politics* (London: Stockwell, 1934).

and internal revenue was placed in the hands of the American financial adviser, with some powers over the Liberian budget and expenditures. In addition, Liberia was caught between the United States and the League of Nations in connection with the charges of slavery and forced labor. World War II catapulted Liberia into a new prominence, giving it a hitherto nonexistent strategic significance, and the United States became directly involved in the developing and equipping of the country, where before it had normally not been prepared to do more than rescue Liberia in time of crisis.

Mussolini's belatedly imperialist war against Ethiopia presented the United States with baffling choices. Here was an open case of aggression overtly designed to round out the Italian colonial empire. Through their network of alliances and understandings, the European powers came to be involved in the matter; and the League of Nations, shunned by the United States, was ineffectually drawn into the thick of it. The direct concern of the United States with Ethiopia was negligible, and the dominant mood of the country was strongly isolationist. In August 1935, as Italian intentions became unmistakably clear, Congress adopted a Neutrality Resolution which imposed a mandatory embargo on the export of "arms, ammunition, or implements of war" for the use of belligerents upon the President's proclamation of the outbreak of war, a step taken on October 5. The League's hesitant moves toward sanctions gave little encouragement to official appeals to Americans to limit to normal amounts their sales of oil and other items useful for war purposes. In fact, American exports to Italy rose hugely during the early months of the war. Neither the halting of aggression nor the protection of an African state against being overwhelmed by a colonial power was a major factor in American policy. The general desire was for neutrality, plain and simple, rather than for even the "positive nonalignment" which represents the contemporary Afro-Asian position.

It was only as World War II developed that the United States came into direct and extensive contact with Africa. As a State Department spokesman put it in the summer of 1943, in one of the exceedingly rare official speeches dealing with Africa prior to the 1950's, "Never before has the word Africa meant so much to the people of the United States . . . the war has turned a powerful searchlight on Africa, focusing attention on its strategic position." [4] The African continent's participation in the war was, however, very largely passive and at the command of the colonial powers, unchallenged by African nationalism. The revolution which was smoldering under the surface in Africa did not burst so clearly into open flame as to be wholly unmistakable until a decade after the end of the war. In this transitional decade American relations with Africa again receded to what had the look of complacent acceptance of the continent as a European colonial domain.

[4] Address by Henry S. Villard, Assistant Chief of the Division of Near Eastern Affairs of the Department of State (Aug. 19, 1943), Department of State Press Release No. 345 (Aug. 18, 1943). The reference to Africa as a land with "a relatively primitive native population" effectively dates the speech and is one which no responsible official would now dream of making.

In a war of global dimensions, requiring an endless supply of manpower and raw materials, so vast a continent as Africa could not be allowed to stand aside. Hundreds of thousands of Africans were drawn directly into the war effort and were exposed to the West and the white man in a fashion whose revolutionary implications were inescapable. A special circumstance which forced attention to the continent was that as Hitler overran Europe, Africa offered the space in which the Allies could regroup their forces and gather the resources which would one day aid them to re-establish themselves in Europe. For this purpose it was necessary to recapture North Africa and also to win back to Free France the African colonies which had drifted into the camp of Pétain. To meet war needs, as well as for the profit and prestige of Belgium, it was essential that the products of the Belgian Congo, and particularly its minerals, including the newly indispensable uranium, should be kept flowing in to the Allied coffers.

The effects of the war in speeding Africa's emergence as an actor on the world stage in its own right were immense. Africans saw service of a variety of kinds abroad, and European and American military contingents, technicians, and governmental personnel appeared in large numbers in Africa. Landing fields were built for the war's planes; new networks of transport and communication were established; and the new machines and instrumentalities of war were on display. The production of raw materials was stepped up to meet the demand, and new industries came into being as the former suppliers of African needs were cut off. In consequence, the numbers of Africans engaged in salary and wage employment multiplied, as did the numbers of those who poured into the urban centers.

At the same time the colonial regimes in Southeast Asia collapsed under the pressure of the Japanese, leaving behind a sense that the days of empire were close to an end. The Atlantic Charter's proclamation of the right of all people to choose the form of government under which they will live spread far and wide even though Churchill sought to deny its applicability to Britain's dependencies. The wartime weakening of the imperial powers and the enhanced prestige of the Soviet Union worked to undermine the hold of the colonial regimes and to strengthen their opponents. In the imperial centers themselves, new conceptions of the obligations of those responsible for the management of colonies were coming to the fore, leading to the practical application of schemes which the reformist critics of colonialism had long been urging. Thus Britain adopted Colonial Development and Welfare Acts, and began to move toward self-government in West Africa, as in the grant of an African majority in the Gold Coast's Legislative Council. For France the key event was the Brazzaville Conference of January, 1944, at which de Gaulle and leading French colonial authorities (but, characteristically for the time, no Africans) mapped out major elements of the future of the French African domain. While the conference unequivocally banned the notion of self-government and of any development outside the framework of the French Empire, it called for basic reforms in colonial legislation and practice which were shortly introduced under the Fourth Republic.

On the African side full-fledged nationalist movements are barely to be found before the end of the war, and in many instances some years later. The most highly developed movements were those of British West Africa, of which one of the most significant expressions was the West African Students Union in Britain. Among the political leaders of Africa at this time, none was more striking than the American-educated Nigerian, Nnamdi Azikiwe, who was carving out for himself a distinguished and influential career as businessman and journalist but, most of all, as political agitator and organizer. Although it is generally true that Africa's swift sweep to independence was foreseen by almost no one, Zik, as he was universally known, in 1943 submitted to the Colonial Office a memorandum which was amazingly close to the actual timetable of development in its call for Africanization, ten years of representative government and five years of full responsible government, at the end of which Nigeria would come to sovereign independence in association with the British Commonwealth.[5]

Forgetting past unpleasantnesses, the United States made a defense agreement with Liberia early in 1942 which established the formal framework within which the United States, in the course of the war, brought over 5,000 troops to the country, installed Roberts Field as a major air station, built roads and artificial ports, and laid some of the foundations for Liberian development.

In the course of the war American trade with Africa went up spectacularly as the ability of Europe to maintain its established economic relations with Africa was impaired. As against a total annual American trade with Africa of less than $250 million in the prewar years, the "five year trade average (1941–1945) brought a 400 per cent increase and an aggregate average annual value of $1,058,523,000." [6] In the same period, American investment in Africa also rose, but not to the same degree. Then, as now, European trade and European capital were well out ahead of their American counterparts.

Within the United States interest in Africa was growing, particularly among the Negroes for whom W.E.B. Du Bois remained the outstanding and indefatigable leader. The number of African students coming to the United States was on the rise, in part through the influence of Azikiwe who saw to it that some of them went to Lincoln University which he had himself attended. Indeed, one Nigerian student is cited as saying at the close of the war: "the first skirmishes in the struggle for political freedom of the 21 million people of Nigeria are being fought today in the colleges of the United States." [7]

[5] See James S. Coleman, *Nigeria, Background to Nationalism* (Berkeley: California University, 1958), pp. 240-41. Azikiwe's views were spelled out in his *Political Blueprint of Nigeria* (Lagos: African Book Co., Ltd., 1943).

[6] Lawrence C. Howard, "The United States and Africa: Trade and Investment," in *Africa Seen by American Negroes* (Dijon: 1958).

[7] See Coleman, *Nigeria*, p. 244. One of Azikiwe's rivals for political leadership in Nigeria, Obafemi Awolowo, wrote that the question as to whether Nigeria should aim for independence or self-government "had never received the attention it deserved until the people of the United States of America forced it into prominence." (*Path to Nigerian Freedom*. London: Faber, 1947, p. 23.)

THE FIRST POSTWAR DECADE

It was a reasonable expectation that once the United States had become as much involved with Africa as it had during the war, it would maintain its ties in the postwar years, but this did not prove to be the case. In the first decade after the war the United States in fact tended to lose touch with Africa again at the official level and moved back in only as the independence of the Sudan in 1956 and of Ghana in 1957 made it clear that the continent was undergoing a fundamental political revolution. Despite occasional wartime warnings to the colonial powers by American spokesmen that the United States was not fighting to preserve their empires, after the war Washington was neither prepared nor interested to challenge the rule of its European allies in Africa south of the Sahara.

American policy and its effects in the postwar decade are difficult to assess with accuracy, in part because some of the facts of the case are concealed in diplomatic archives, but also in part because the policy wavered between acceptance of self-determination and a cautious conservatism dictated by America's global postwar position and in particular by the spell the Cold War cast over all of Washington's deliberations. American enthusiasm for the anticolonial cause appears to have been greater during the war and in its immediate aftermath than three or four years later. Furthermore, it is often impossible to tell whether the colonies of Black Africa were seriously meant to be included when proposals were made for a drastic overhaul of colonial rule or for a prompt move toward independence, or whether people actually had in mind territories in Asia, the Middle East, and North Africa which more urgently called for action. It was easy to regard the African colonies as being in safe hands: any upsetting of the applecart could send the apples rolling away where the ever-active Communists could gather them up. The counterargument was that Communism was most likely to spread among disaffected peoples denied their freedom, but the United States appeared to see it as the safer course not to disturb the existing order in Africa. The colonial powers nonetheless felt that they were under pressure from the United States to hasten on toward independence, although there is little, if any, evidence that Washington interceded on behalf of sub-Saharan African colonies prior to the Kennedy administration. It seems more nearly correct to assume that the United States followed after Britain, France, and Belgium as they introduced reforms and then conceded independence to their colonies than that it sought to hasten them on. The British creation of an African unofficial majority in the Gold Coast Legislative Council in 1946, for example, went at least as far as the United States was likely to suggest.

Unquestionably during the war the United States was in an anticolonial mood, deriving in part from old-established tradition and in part from contemplating the ease with which Japan had toppled over colonial regimes in Southeast Asia. Washington urged Britain to speed India's freedom and France and the Netherlands to change their ways in Indochina and Indonesia, while North Africa was nudged to assert itself. One of the key contributions of the United States to the shaping of the UN Charter lay in the demand for colonial accountability which came to be embodied for all non-self-governing territories in Chapter XI. The tightening up of international control in the trusteeship system which replaced the League's mandates also owed much to the United States. Another matter which sustained the postwar image of American anticolonialism was the role played in the complex negotiations concerning the fate of the Italian colonies, and most notably the effort to draw upon the new conception in the UN Charter of a trusteeship which would be exercised by the UN itself. In line with the plea of Secretary of State Cordell Hull during the war that the colonial powers should "fix, at the earliest practicable moment, dates upon which the colonial peoples would be accorded the status of full independence within a system of general security," [8] the United States backed time limits for the Italian colonies, and a ten year period was indeed set for Somaliland. An illustration of the decline in American anticolonial zeal can be found in the episode in 1955 when the American representative on the UN Visiting Mission to Tanganyika endorsed the request for a twenty-five year timetable for Tanganyikan independence, but at a later stage was forced by Washington to withdraw his rash move, despite its own precedent in the Philippines. How rash it was is demonstrated by the fact that Tanganyika achieved its independence not in twenty-five but in six years.

American abstention from involvement in African affairs could be justified on the ground that Africa appeared relatively calm and untroubled. Thus in a speech in May, 1950, George McGhee, Assistant Secretary of State for Near Eastern, South Asian, and African Affairs, singled out Africa as one place "where—in the broadest sense—no crisis exists," and he expressed his gratification at being able to find "a region of 10 million square miles in which no significant inroads have been made by Communism and to be able to characterize the area as relatively stable and secure." [9] Since Africa's stability and security were obviously products of colonial rule, it was evident that the United States rated the absence of a crisis more highly than an attack upon the European colonialism which served in fact as a welcome bulwark against the allegedly greater evil of Communism.

Official American policy was discreetly restrained in its advocacy of an overhauling of the African colonial structure, but private American individuals and groups of many kinds were discovering Africa in constantly growing numbers, and the Department of State was expanding its corps of persons familiar with Africa. In academic circles a new interest was being shown in Africa, manifested in an increase in courses dealing with the continent, in research on African themes, and in the founding of African programs or study centers. African art and music attracted unprecedented attention. At the same time, new and enhanced attention was given to Africa by American newspapers and magazines, although even at

[8] Cordell Hull, *The Memoirs of Cordell Hull* (New York: Macmillan, 1948), II, 1235.

[9] Department of State Bulletin, XXII (June 19, 1950), 999-1002. Mr. McGhee pleaded that the crisis-free time be used to deepen American interest in, and study of, Africa.

the present day the number of American correspondents in Africa is dismayingly small. Both officially and privately what was going on in Africa came under far closer scrutiny than before, and a body of Americans competent in African affairs grew up more rapidly than could have been anticipated. In this whole process, the American Foundations—including such giants as Ford, Rockefeller, and Carnegie, and many smaller ones as well—made a vital contribution through the projects and persons they supported. As more and more Americans, both official and private, went to Africa, the pressure on the European authorities inevitably grew, even though what was said and done may at no point have represented formal governmental policy.

What was involved was well brought out in 1956 by Chester Bowles in his book, *Africa's Challenge to the United States*. "The most powerful country in the world, which asserts that it is leading a global coalition for freedom," he contended, "cannot declare itself to be a nonparticipant in the affairs of a continent boiling with change, without abdicating its position of leadership." [10] Finding many officials advocating that the United States should have no positive African policy because such a policy would bring it into conflict with its European allies, Bowles protested that this put Americans in the position of being regarded as blundering sentimentalists by the colonial powers and as timid hypocrites by African nationalists. The result was to antagonize both and win the respect of neither.

The American swing toward active public advocacy of self-determination for African peoples did not, in fact, take place until the movement toward independence was well under way. Obeisance was paid to the principle of self-determination, but it was a principle to be cautiously observed and with emphasis on securing an *orderly* transition. As late as May, 1959, when the sweep toward a new Africa was in full swing, the Assistant Secretary of State for African Affairs, Joseph C. Satterthwaite, continued to stress the same cautious line:

> We support African political aspirations where they are moderate, non-violent and constructive and take into account their obligations to and interdependence with the world community. We also support the principle of continued African ties with Western Europe. We see no reason why there should be a conflict between these two concepts.[11]

These are, of course, wholly unobjectionable, safe and sane statements of policy, but sadly unimaginative and uncreative. What African nationalist would throw his hat in the air on hearing them? Secretary Dulles himself contended in November, 1953, that the United States was pushing for independence more than appeared on the surface, but added that where restraint was exercised, it was because of a reasoned conviction that "precipitate action would in fact not produce independence but only transition to a captivity far worse than present dependence." [12] The African

---

[10] *Africa's Challenge to the United States* (Berkeley and Los Angeles: University of California, 1956), pp. 96-97.
[11] Department of State Press Release, No. 298 (May 1, 1959).
[12] Department of State Bulletin, XXIX, No. 753 (Nov. 30, 1953).

nationalist, however, was in no mood to accept this characteristic American warning of the dangers of precipitate action and was unconcerned about the risk of a "far worse" Communist captivity if he could only get his present captors off his back. The American fascination with the menace of Communism impaired the ability to understand what moved the African political leaders and to establish sympathetic and mutually satisfactory relations with them.

For sub-Saharan Africa, the most significant turning point was the transformation of the Gold Coast into the independent state of Ghana in 1957 under the dynamic and ambitious leadership of Kwame Nkrumah, dramatically released from jail in 1951 to become Leader of Government Business and in the succeeding year Prime Minister. By the mid-1950's Nigeria was clearly on the way, through regional self-government, toward the independence which she secured in 1960. For the French territories, the culminating point of the postwar reforms was the *loi cadre* of 1956 which made possible a great extension of self-government. Following in the footsteps of Guinea which alone opted for independence in 1958, the remainder of the French dependencies, except French Somaliland, achieved their independence in 1960.

The tardiness of the United States in promoting this unprecedented rush to create new states is well indicated by Vernon McKay who remarks, perhaps somewhat overoptimistically, in the course of a detailed investigation of American pronouncements on self-determination at this period that:

> By the time Britain took the crucial, precedent-setting step of giving independence to Ghana on March 6, 1957, it was obvious to even the most conservative officials that the United States could not be more royalist than the Queen.[13]

THE UNITED STATES ADJUSTS TO AFRICAN INDEPENDENCE

It is impossible to set any precise date for a drastic shift in American policy toward Africa, principally because no drastic shift occurred, but also because the processes of adjustment were gradual. At no point was American policy starkly reactionary nor did it ever turn radically anticolonial; the trend was always toward the middle of the road with deviations to the right or the left. The intensification of African nationalism and the growing readiness of Britain, France, and Belgium to yield to it forced the United States to run to catch up with a procession which it would have liked to believe it was leading. The outside limits of the transition can be set at, say, 1955 at one end and the start of the Kennedy administration in 1961 at the other. A closer reckoning would place it between 1956 and 1958. American policy was engaged in a gradual process of change during President Eisenhower's second term as official spokesmen edged cautiously away from warnings against the dangers of premature independence toward acceptance of the fact that colonialism was ending. It should not be forgotten that the repudiation of British and French intervention in the Suez crisis came in the middle of Eisenhower's Presidency.

[13] Vernon McKay, *Africa in World Politics* (New York: Harper 1963), pp. 322-23.

What may be regarded as both an outstanding symbol and a major instrument of change was what was taking place in the structure of the Department of State in relation to the handling of African affairs in their own right and not as colonially subsidiary to Europe.[14] The new significance of Africa for the United States in World War II was recognized when a separate office for Africa was set up in 1943 in the Near Eastern division. The next major move was the establishment in 1956 of a semi-autonomous Office of African Affairs, divided into two branches for North Africa and Africa south of the Sahara and headed by a Deputy Assistant Secretary of State for African Affairs. In 1958 Africa came fully into its own in the Department when Congress authorized the creation of a separate Bureau of African Affairs endowed with its own Assistant Secretary of State, although battles still remained to be fought with the old-established and prestige-laden European desks. Public attention was attracted to the new Assistant Secretaryship when President-elect Kennedy, even prior to naming Dean Rusk as his Secretary of State, announced his selection of G. Mennen Williams, oft-time Governor of Michigan and a vigorous champion of liberal causes, to take over the African post.

A corresponding change of great importance for American relations with Africa was the replacing of the handful of unenterprising American consulates in Africa by a growing number of embassies, equipped with information and aid staffs, as the colonial territories came to independence. McKay has brought forward the striking statistic that "the United States Foreign Service had 256 officers in the single country of West Germany in 1957 in contrast to only 248 officers in the whole of Africa." This imbalance was shortly rectified, but it was no easy task to seek to remedy virtually overnight the grievous shortage of Americans knowledgeable about Africa.

Among the Americans interested in Africa no group was more significant or more deeply affected than the Negroes, whose relationship to Africa had always been in some part ambiguous. The emergence of independent African states inevitably drew their attention to that continent and to their distinctive ancestry, although it by no means necessarily reduced the element of ambiguity. Far more than sheer coincidence in time linked the anticolonial upsurge of Africa to the civil rights movement and the drive against segregation in the United States. The stature of the Negro in America was enhanced by the existence of a number of African states taking their sovereign place in the world community. Furthermore, the dimensions and nature of the American racial problem were strongly affected by the reverse flow of substantial numbers of Africans to the United States who came in one or another diplomatic capacity, in the African embassies which sprang up in Washington, in connection with the UN or other international agencies or conferences, and as students in American colleges and universities. The appearance on the American scene of this body of Africans, insistent on their right to

[14] For a more elaborate examination, see McKay, *Africa*, Chap. 16, from which the following account has been adapted. See also McKay's "The African Operations of United States Government Agencies," in *The United States and Africa*, rev. ed., Walter Goldschmidt, ed. (New York: Praeger, 1963), pp. 273-95.

equal and dignified treatment, pressed home the fact that the United States could not live in the new world of color in its old, accustomed ways. The ferment of Africa and the ferment of the Negro American could not possibly be kept separate from each other in watertight compartments.[15]

As Ghana's coming to independence in 1957 is taken as the watershed on this side of which all streams flowed away from colonialism, so the report of Vice-President Nixon on his presence at Ghana's independence celebration and his visit to half a dozen other African countries symbolically marks a turning point for the United States.[16] This report, despite a regrettable inability to escape making "the conflict between the forces of freedom and international communism" its repeated central theme, was insistent upon the importance of Africa to the United States. The Vice-President included a number of recommendations, such as a stepping up of State Department and diplomatic concern with Africa, an attack upon racial discrimination at home, and an expansion of economic links.

In line with later developments, he recommended that the United States should encourage the continuance of special ties between African and European countries where these were considered mutually advantageous and, in particular, that the United States should not take on singlehanded the task of providing economic assistance.

For the double reason that Africa had not been a crisis area and that America's allies remained in colonial control of most of it, only minimal bounty had trickled to that continent from the American aid programs. As independent African states began to take over from the colonial regimes, however, the African share increased rapidly, even though the sums allocated to Africa continued to be a small segment of total American foreign aid. An indication of the new American appreciation of the African scene can be secured from a glance at the figures for the critical years of Africa's political advance. In the four years, fiscal 1953-1957, loans and grants of only $120.3 million were made to Africa under the Mutual Security Act. The succeeding years brought regular increases: in 1958 to $82.4 million; in 1959 to $149.8 million, and in 1960 to $169.7 million, reaching a peak of loans and grants of $315 million in 1962.[17]

Enough has already been said to make it clear that in President Eisenhower's second term the transformation of Africa from colonialism to independence was evoking a significant American response. The importance which had come to be attached to Africa was at least twice signaled by

[15] See Rupert Emerson and Martin Kilson, "The American Dilemma in a Changing World: The Rise of Africa and the Negro American," *Dædalus*, Vol. 94, No. 4 (Fall, 1965).

[16] Richard Nixon, *The Emergence of Africa, Report to the President by Vice-President Nixon on His Trip to Africa* (Washington: Department of State, April, 1957).

[17] See *U.S. Overseas Loans and Grants and Assistance from International Organizations, Obligations and Loan Authorizations July 1, 1945-June 30, 1965*, Special Report Prepared for the House Foreign Affairs Committee by the Agency for International Development, March 18, 1966, p. 73. The full American economic assistance figure would include such other items as Food for Peace and Export-Import Bank loans.

the President in the course of his last year in office. Early in 1960 in his Mutual Security message to Congress he asked for a special allocation of $20 million to Africa to meet "an imperative and immediate requirement for increased education and training." On September 22, 1960, he addressed the UN General Assembly which in that session was uniquely preoccupied with African matters, including the admission of no less than sixteen African states. In this speech, he laid out a five-point program for Africa which was strongly influenced by the special difficulties of the Congo but which also constituted a broad statement of American policy toward the continent.[18] Insistent that "the international community protect the newly emerging nations of Africa from outside pressures that threaten their independence and sovereign rights," he called for help in assuring the security of African states without wasteful and dangerous competition in arms, emergency aid to the Congo, international assistance in shaping long-term development programs, and an all-out UN effort in the educational sphere.

The accession to the presidency of John F. Kennedy gave promise of an even more drastic overhaul of American policy toward Africa than had been undertaken in the last years of his predecessor's tenure. Where Eisenhower's regime had borne a conservative stamp on the whole, Kennedy seized the occasion of his inaugural address to proclaim that Americans were the heirs of a revolution which should be pressed forward. It was remembered that in 1957 he had made, to French indignation, an appeal for self-determination in Algeria in far more forthright terms than most public figures employ when talking of the affairs of a friendly country. As the presidential campaign of 1960 came nearer, he protested the American habit of abstaining in the UN on votes on colonial issues, stressing the bitterness with which the colonial peoples looked upon their white rulers. Speaking in the Senate on June 14, 1960, he called for a great increase in the American effort to encourage the newly emerging African countries and pointed out that in a few years they would control one-quarter of the votes in the UN General Assembly. Attacking the narrow self-interest which would seek to use Africans only as pawns in the Cold War, he asserted:

> We can no longer afford policies which refuse to accept the inevitable triumph of nationalism in Africa, the inevitable end of colonialism, and, fortunately, colonialism will end not only in Africa, but, in the long run, resistance to colonialism and the rise of nationalism will be the basic influences which will undermine the great Communist colonial empire.[19]

Although the honeymoon period of American relations remained substantially unimpaired during the latter part of the Eisenhower administra-

[18] For the text, see *Documents on American Foreign Relations, 1960*, ed. Richard P. Stebbins (New York: Council on Foreign Relations, 1961), pp. 552-55.

[19] *Ibid.*, p. 67. Arthur Schlesinger, Jr., reports that in the index of Kennedy's 1960 campaign speeches there were 479 references to Africa, centering on the theme that "we have lost ground in Africa because we have neglected and ignored the needs and aspirations of the African people," *A Thousand Days* (Boston: Houghton, 1965), p. 554.

tion, African leaders looked forward eagerly to the new regime which was taking over in Washington, with the expectation that they would now find a more liberally sympathetic response on the American side. With Kennedy as President, the United States was fully launched on its new relationship with the new Africa.

4

United States Interests
and Activities in Africa

The American concern with Africa in every sphere has been increasing rapidly in recent years, but concrete and identifiable American interests in the continent always have been and continue to be slight. In no major segment of the world has the United States had so small a measure of involvement as in Africa.[1] An unduly derogatory but not completely misleading version might classify the American concern as being primarily negative in character; i.e., that the American national interest assigns no vital place to Africa in its scheme of things, but would suffer if Africa were to fall into hostile hands. Even taking into account the African origin of an important fraction of the American people, it remains the fact that the present intensification of relations between Africa and the United States set off from a very low level of mutual acquaintance and still rests on fragile and uncertain foundations.

It is evident that the United States could not have vested interests in, or traditional ties with, most of the African states, since almost all of them emerged from colonialism into independent existence only in the last few years, and during the colonial era the United States had achieved virtually nothing in the way of distinctive relations with any of them. The

[1] For a diametrically opposite view, see *Renmin Ribao* [Jenmin Jih Pao], editorial translated in *The Peking Review*, VII, No. 16 (April 17, 1964), 9: "Africa is an important economic base for the very existence of West European and North American imperialist and colonialist countries, which rob the continent of its rich natural resources and exploit its vast manpower. Because of its geographical position and its many strategic minerals and raw materials, Africa holds a vital place in the war and aggression plans of the imperialist camp, headed by the United States."

two outstanding exceptions were Liberia, with which the United States had its special relationship, and South Africa, which was increasingly a center for American trade and investment. For the rest it was a matter of building new connections from the ground up, inevitably relying at the outset on general principles and doctrines rather than on considerations specific to the particular country.

The present political importance of Africa to the United States as to other major powers is greatly enhanced by the special conditions which now characterize international relations. Apart from the fact that the globe has notoriously shrunk, bringing all peoples and problems more intimately into one another's laps, the two most important elements are the existence of the Cold War and of the UN. Intrinsically, the specific gravity of the African states as political forces on the world scene is very slight: they possess, in fact, almost none of the attributes which one would normally associate with a power, and their human and material potentialities, whether for peace or war, are still only meagerly developed. The fragmentation of the continent into many states, the newness and shakiness of the political institutions of most of them, their low economic level, and their military insignificance inevitably leave Africa still rather in the position of being acted upon by the rest of the world than reaching out itself to act on others. Of the African countries south of the Sahara (and without much additional qualification, north of the Sahara as well) only South Africa has produced a highly developed economy, superimposed by the white community on the African subsistence economy, a tight-knit and efficient political system, and a well-trained and well-equipped modern military force.

Whatever the relative impotence and passiveness of Africa, however, the pressures of the Cold War operate in such fashion as to create a marked sensitivity on the part of Washington, Moscow, and Peking to any change in the global balance or to any rift in the status quo which makes such change likely or feasible. In such circumstances Africa, just coming out from under colonialism, is an obvious target for Cold War attention by all interested parties. Overnight, yesterday's backwater colonial capitals have become centers of international concern and intrigue. The Cold War pressures have stopped short of attempting to enlist African countries overtly in political-military pacts, but the obvious intent is to win their informal allegiance or at least to persuade them to deny their favors to the opposing camp.

Even without the Cold War, membership in the UN would give the African states an international importance which they would otherwise not have. To pick random examples, the opinion of Burundi on the limitation of armaments or of Upper Volta on Indonesia's "confrontation" of Malaysia would be of virtually no international consequence and probably would not even be formulated if each did not have a UN vote. Leaving aside the highly debatable question as to whether this is a sensible way to run an international system, it remains the fact that the African states as well as a number of other small UN members are endowed with a voting strength utterly out of keeping with any principle save the peculiar parody of democracy which calls for "one state, one vote." This situation ensures that the African states will be wooed by all suitors who have an interest in the outcome of UN deliberations.

The strategic significance of Africa is obviously dependent on what kind of war is being fought by whom. It is highly unlikely that in the foreseeable future African states will themselves produce military forces which could seriously affect the international balance, but the vast territory which they occupy and the raw materials which they control might give the continent an unexpected significance. Despite its involvement with Africa during World War II, the United States does not now appear to take a very active interest in Africa's strategic potentialities, nor has it engaged in any serious way in the arming of African countries. The one defense agreement into which the United States has entered in Africa was made in 1959 with Liberia and provides that if Liberia is threatened by aggression, its government and that of the United States will immediately consult as to what action may be appropriate. A small military assistance program has been undertaken in Liberia and in a scattering few other African countries with Ethiopia and, more recently, the Congo as the major recipients. The relinquishing of air bases in Morocco under nationalist pressure left Wheelus Field in Libya as the only surviving American base on the African continent, but space tracking facilities have also been established in South Africa, Nigeria, and Madagascar, and a communications center in Ethiopia.

It may well be that the greatest potential military significance of Africa for the United States is neither the strength of its armed forces nor its utility as a base of operations and source of supply but the danger that racial or Cold War complications might cause the involvement of American forces on the continent as they have already become involved in Korea and Vietnam.

If the present military-strategic concern of the United States in Africa is minimal and largely negative in character, the American economic stake is larger and more positive, but it represents only a small proportion of America's foreign economic interests. Trade and investment have grown continually in recent years, but they remain of marginal importance to the American economy. The role of Africa as a major supplier of American needs in particular commodities has been summed up by Andrew M. Kamarck in the following terms:

> Africa supplies the bulk of our consumption of diamonds (industrial and gem), columbium, cobalt, corundum, pyrethrum, arabic gum, wattle bark and extract, palm and palm kernel oil; at least half of our consumption of cocoa, cloves, vanilla beans, extra long staple cotton, mahogany logs, long fiber asbestos; and around a quarter of our consumption of antimony, chrome, graphite, manganese, tantalum, goat and kid skins, papain, and canary seeds.[2]

To this list must be added very substantial purchases of coffee, for the most part from East Africa and Angola, of rubber from Liberia and

[2] "The African Economy and International Trade" in *The United States and Africa*, rev. ed., Walter Goldschmidt, ed. (New York: Praeger, 1963), p. 157.

Nigeria, and of gold and uranium, primarily from South Africa. Despite the importance of a number of the items which are derived from Africa, it was Mr. Kamarck's conclusion not only that the United States could get along without them, but also that the elimination of both imports from Africa and of African markets for American exports would cause only an imperceptible ripple in our standard of living. He predicted, however, that the economic interest of the United States in Africa is likely to grow in the future since the American need for imported raw materials is sure to become more and more pressing as domestic supplies are depleted. African production may be expected to increase as the continent is developed and as new mineral deposits are discovered and opened up, but expanding markets for some of its agricultural staples such as cocoa, coffee, cotton, and tobacco, and even some of its minerals may be difficult to find. As far as American exports to Africa are concerned, although foodstuffs—notably grain and grain preparations—have been a surprisingly large element, much of the trade has consisted of machinery, automobiles, chemicals, manufactures, and textiles. As African development advances, the demand for such products should constantly grow.

For present purposes, however, it remains the fact that Africa is not economically vital to the United States. The far greater economic stake which America's allies in Europe have in Africa must often be of more concern to Washington than the direct involvement of the United States itself.

THE TRADE OF THE UNITED STATES WITH AFRICA

American trade with Africa has risen consistently but not spectacularly in the last decades, expanding slightly more rapidly than the total American foreign trade. Table 1 shows American trade with the entire African continent and with the world at large (000 omitted).[3]

TABLE 1 • U.S. TRADE WITH AFRICA AND THE WORLD, 1936-1964

	U.S. exports to Africa	U.S. imports from Africa	Total U.S. exports	Total U.S. imports
1936-40 (av.)	132,068	81,220	3,219,581	2,482,030
1950	369,212	493,661	10,275,043	8,852,161
1955	622,838	619,352	15,547,074	11,384,436
1960	765,782	534,380	20,549,683	14,653,929
1963	992,158	777,452	23,344,857	17,137,923
1964	1,218,471	916,693	26,438,368	18,684,633

American exports to Africa in 1964 were 4.6 per cent of total American exports, and American imports from Africa were 4.9 per cent of total American imports, whereas in 1960 the comparable figures were 4 per cent and 3.7 per cent. Coming at the matter from the other side, it has been calculated that in 1964 the United States took 9.1 per cent of Africa's exports and supplied 11.4 per cent of the continent's imports. The British

[3] Both tables in this section and the immediately following material are taken from the relevant issues of the *Statistical Abstract of the United States*, issued by the U.S. Bureau of the Census.

and French share in both categories ranged from 17 per cent to 19 per cent.[4]

South Africa has, with temporary fluctuations, consistently held something like a third of the total African trade with the United States in both directions, although it has normally bought more from the United States than it has sold. Thus in 1955 American exports to South Africa were valued at $268,590,000 while the imports from South Africa came to $95,-566,000; in 1960 the comparable figures were $277,297,000 and $107,990,-000; and in 1964 $392,679,000 and $249,466,000. The trade of the several North African countries, including the Sudan, has been even more heavily weighted than that of South Africa on the side of purchases from the United States; in 1960 American exports to North Africa came to $278,-553,000 and its imports from that area to only $49,679,000, the comparable figures for 1964 being $464,684,000 and $63,151,000. Added together, South Africa and the North African countries have of late absorbed more than two-thirds of the total value of American exports to Africa, while their share of African imports to the United States has been between one third and one half.[5]

The trade balance is somewhat rectified by the fact that the African countries south of the Sahara and north of South Africa have contributed much more heavily to imports to the United States than they have drawn on American exports,[6] the West African share in both categories being much greater than that of East Africa. For these purposes West Africa has been interpreted to reach as far south as the Congo and Angola, and East Africa to embrace the entire territory from Ethiopia to the erstwhile Rhodesia-Nyasaland Federation, including Mozambique and Madagascar. The position of these two regions of sub-Saharan Africa in American trade is shown in Table 2.

TABLE 2 • U.S. TRADE WITH WEST AND EAST AFRICA, 1955-1964

	U.S. exports to		U.S. imports from	
	West Africa	East Africa	West Africa	East Africa
1955	$152,711	$33,910	$321,237	$87,514
1960	161,111	34,186	268,175	92,093
1963	256,643	45,102	303,365	137,145
1964	288,232	50,106	412,832	165,948

AMERICAN INVESTMENT IN AFRICA

As in the case of trade, American private investment in Africa has increased rapidly in recent years, but it is much smaller than the European investment in the continent and is only a small fraction of the total American private foreign investment. Since the colonial authorities were generally unreceptive to large-scale American economic penetration and

[4] Anthony Astrachan, "Les Intérêts Economiques des Etats-Unis en Afrique," Le Mois en Afrique, No. 3 (May, 1966), p. 58.
[5] Statistical Abstract, 1965, pp. 884-85.
[6] In 1965 a nonprofit Afro-American Purchasing Center, Inc., initiated and supported by AID, was formed to promote an expansion of American exports to Africa (The New York Times, August 20, 1965).

sought to preserve their dependent domains for themselves, the Union of South Africa and Liberia were the two major areas for American investment. South Africa, in particular, despite official denunciations of its apartheid doctrine, has continued to be attractive to American capital.

In 1950, American direct investment in the whole of Africa was estimated to account for $352,400,000 of a total American foreign direct investment of $11,788,000,000 or 3 per cent. Some three-fifths of the African investment was in South Africa and Liberia, valued respectively at $140,100,000 and $82,000,000, while Egypt came third with $39,300,000. Between 1950 and 1958 the American investment in Africa more than doubled, but it was still under 3 per cent of the total foreign investment. By 1960 American investment in Africa had risen to just over the billion dollar mark, but at the same time the global American foreign investment had climbed to nearly $35,000,000,000. The latest available figures show a continued rise in the American investment in Africa which in 1965 came to $1,904,000,000, but this still represented only 3.8 per cent of the total American investment abroad of $49,217,000,000. It could legitimately be acclaimed as reaching a new high point for American private capital in Africa, but it only barely exceeded the American investment of $1,677,-000,000 in Australia and faded into insignificance beside the investment in Canada of $15,172,000,000 and in Latin America of $9,371,000,000. Among the African countries South Africa continued to head the list with an American investment officially estimated at $528,000,000.[7]

Despite appeals from American authorities for greater boldness on the part of American businessmen in seizing the opportunity to invest in Africa and the assurances given by a number of African governments that they welcome such investment, the American investor has so far displayed no great interest in most of the continent, save for its southern tip. Apart from South Africa, the major American investments in Africa have been in the extractive industries, involving the opening and exploiting of mineral resources, and in different branches of the petroleum industry. Relatively very little private American capital has gone into other branches of economic development which would diversify the productive facilities of African countries, open up transport and communciations, and provide needed services. Although under appropriate contractual arrangements foreign-financed mining may make a substantial addition to a country's resources, at its worst its contribution can be negligible as the lion's share of the profit is drained off abroad, a subsistence wage is paid to the indigenous work force, and the basic mineral resources of the country are exhausted.

The failure of American entrepreneurs to take a more active and extensive interest in Africa's potentialities derives from several factors, including both the ability to make a handsome profit at home and the limitations imposed on the African market by poverty and smallness of scale. Africa is remote, still relatively little known, and in varying degrees, hazardous. It is, inevitably, a continent in flux, with many basic adjustments

[7] Samuel Pizer and Frederick Cutler, "Foreign Investments, 1965-66," *Survey of Current Business,* September, 1966, p. 34.

still to be made before the transition from colonialism to independence can be regarded as complete. If the turmoil of the Congo has not been repeated elsewhere, there have been a number of "incidents," coups, and assassinations. The assurances of good will on the part of African governments toward foreign investors have often been accompanied, rightly enough, by warnings as to the way in which alien enterprises are expected to conduct themselves. In many African countries there is an open or underlying hostility toward capitalism in general and alien capital in particular: the Leninist doctrine that imperialism is a product of capitalism has found wide acceptance. Whatever the varied meanings which may be attached to the idea of African socialism, most of the African states regard themselves as socialist. Exploitation by alien capitalist interests can easily be interpreted as the essence of colonialism, and the menace of neo-colonialist domination through foreign investment is portrayed as a constant threat. In such a setting and given the nationalist drive of the new countries, a resort to nationalization or the harassment of foreign enterprises and entrepreneurs must always loom up as a possibility. The ambivalence which is involved is peculiarly well illustrated in the case of Ghana, which has both welcomed and denounced alien capital. The high regard in which Nigeria has been held by the American authorities and, in lesser degree, by American investors, derived in part from its acceptance of the legitimacy of the private enterprise system.

For many Africans who have come to acquaintance with the modern world, the desire to speed economic development by every means, including encouragement of foreign investment and enterprise, is constantly subject to being checked by the numbing fear that alien capital will again take over the substance of colonial control.

AMERICAN AID TO AFRICA

The American aid program for Africa did not get seriously under way until the political transformation of the continent was no longer susceptible of doubt. There could be no dispute about the earlier need of the African countries and peoples for assistance to speed and amplify the movement toward development started by the colonial regimes, but the United States had little direct concern, and the metropolitan powers did not welcome foreign intrusion into their colonial domains. The coming of independence drastically changed the situtation. The new countries were eager not only to secure economic and technical assistance, but also to exercise their new-found freedom to enter into international relationships on their own outside the colonial framework. The frowns of the former colonial authorities could no longer be decisive even though the United States strove to avoid any impression that it was elbowing its allies aside in their former domains. A prime incentive for an expansion of the American aid program was furnished by the evident interest of the Communist powers in making their way into a vast continent which had been previously closed to them. However grieved the Africans may have been to see the Cold War overflowing into their continent, they stood to profit from the international rivalries which it brought, and nowhere, with the partial exception of the Congo, has it so far come to an open confrontation between the opposing sides, despite much sharp rivalry for influence.

Three distinguishing characteristics of the American aid operations in Africa are that they have been held down to modest proportions, that the military element has been slight, and that as a general rule they were deliberately made supplementary to those of the former colonial powers. A committee on aid policy appointed by President Kennedy and headed by General Clay reported early in 1963 that since immediate security interests were less evident in Africa than in countries adjacent to the Communist bloc and close ties had been maintained with the metropoles, the committee regarded Africa "as an area where the Western European countries should logically bear most of the necessary aid burden." Although this injunction has been generally heeded, several important exceptions have been made to it for special reasons in such cases as those of the Congo, Guinea, Sudan, Ghana, and Nigeria. Where it has been applied, as in most of the former French territories, the inevitable result has been to detract from the independent role of the United States. While this policy presumably had the desired effect of encouraging the flow of aid from the ex-colonial powers, it also perpetuated relationships which all too easily lend themselves to charges of neo-colonialism.

The slow start and the relatively trifling sums involved in the early days are reflected in the calculation that from 1945 to 1955 the United States had given away without requirement of repayment a total of $46.1 billion, of which Africa as a whole received 0.15 per cent ($71 million plus small sums transferred by European metropolitan countries to their colonies from their Marshall Plan receipts). Of this $71 million, more than $70 million went to Liberia, Egypt, Ethiopia, and Libya, an indication of the trifling share of the colonial territories. In the same ten years the United States loaned to all countries a total of $161.1 billion, of which African entities received $342.8 million (2.12 per cent). White-dominated South Africa and Rhodesia were the major beneficiaries of these loan funds. South Africa borrowed $151.8 million from the Export-Import Bank, a commercial rather than an aid transaction; the Rhodesian Federation borrowed $60.7 million; Liberia, $44.8 million; Egypt, Ethiopia, and Morocco, a total of $75.8 million, leaving only an insignificant amount for the rest of Africa.[8]

Following Ghana's independence in 1957, the American aid program for Africa began to climb upward. In fiscal year 1962 a peak was reached with AID loans and grants of $315 million, supplemented by $105 million under the Food for Peace program, and $67 million in Export-Import Bank loans. The decline which then set in is reflected in the figures for fiscal year 1965 when AID loans and grants came to only $149.8 million, Food for Peace to $117.3 million, and Export-Import Bank loans to $34.5 million. Despite the increase in American aid to Africa after 1957, the continent continued to have a relatively small share of the

[8] The Honorable Francis P. Bolton, *Report of the Special Study Mission to Africa, South and East of the Sahara,* printed for the use of the House Committee on Foreign Affairs, 84th Cong., 2nd sess. (Washington: Govt. Printing Office, 1956), pp. 129-30.

total funds disbursed, decreasing from 10.1 per cent in fiscal year 1962 to 6.7 per cent in fiscal year 1965. Limitations imposed by the fact that Africa was not a crisis area nor one in which the United States had urgent interests and that it retained special ties to Europe were strikingly reflected in the allocation of only $1.5 billion to the entire continent by AID and its predecessor agencies from 1948 to 1964 whereas Korea alone was allotted $2.4 billion and Vietnam $1.9 billion in the same period, apart from huge direct military assistance to both countries.[9]

American military assistance programs for Africa have intentionally been held to a low level in order to minimize the danger of an arms race. From 1948 to 1965 the military aid program for all of Africa totaled only $186.1 million of a global total of $34.7 billion. The major African recipient of military assistance in this period was Ethiopia, which secured aid valued at $95.6 million, while Morocco came in a poor second-best with $31.9 million.[10] The military aid to Ethiopia was officially justified on such grounds as that the country had been helpful to the United States on key international issues, had a stable, moderate government, was becoming a focal point for African development, and, of primary American interest, was the site of the important Defense Department communications facility at Asmara. In the last years, the troubled affairs of the Congo have led to the allocation of substantial military assistance to that country, without which, the American aid authorities have held, it would not have been possible to control the terrorist and guerrilla activities which threatened the legitimate government. The total military assistance received in fiscal year 1965 came to $17.7 million of which $2.3 million went to the Congo and $8.3 million to Ethiopia. In the previous year of a total of $28.4 million in military aid to all of Africa, Ethiopia received $10.3 million and the Congo $5 million.[11]

The shaping of an effective and acceptable aid program for Africa presents exceptional difficulties, even apart from the old-established interests of the former colonial powers and the distance from the Cold War frontiers. The virtually unlimited needs of Africa in every respect raise insoluble problems as to the proper priorities, and a sensible allocation of available aid resources is greatly complicated by the existence of so many states, a number of which give little promise, at the best, of being able to do more than survive at a bare subsistence level. Even if substantial external aid is continued indefinitely, their prospects for development in the progressive terms of the modern world are dishearteningly slim.

[9] These statistics have all been taken from annual and other official Agency for International Development reports, including *U.S. Overseas Loans and Grants and Assistance from International Organizations, Obligations and Loan Authorizations, July 1, 1945-June 30, 1965,* Special Report Prepared for the House Foreign Affairs Committee (1966), and *Proposed Mutual Defense and Development Programs FY 1966: Summary Presentation to the Congress,* prepared by AID and the Department of Defense (Washington: Govt. Printing Office, 1965), Table No. 2, p. 227. See also "U.S. Economic Aid to Africa, 1950-64," *Africa Report,* IX, No. 11 (December, 1964), 8-12.

[10] *U.S. Overseas Loans and Grants,* pp. 73, 82, 95.

[11] *The Foreign Assistance Program, Annual Report to the Congress Fiscal Year 1965* (Washington: Govt. Printing Office, 1966), p. 69.

Illiteracy, disease, poverty, primitive agricultural methods, the lack of such fundamentals as transport and communications and power, and the presence of no more than the rudiments of modern industry—these are the basic conditions of the great bulk of tropical Africa. In most instances, such prerequisites of development as an effective administration, skilled managers and technicians, and a trained labor force are lacking. The foundations on which development can be built have barely been laid, although the colonial regimes in varying degree cleared the ground for them and began the process.

Given the multiplicity of African countries and needs, it is evident that the difficulties in cutting an already not very large aid pie are immense. Although the American aid program has in the past reached out to embrace every independent country on the continent, except South Africa, an effort has increasingly been made to concentrate on a few countries where aid would achieve the most substantial results, a trend strengthened by the review of American aid policy in Africa undertaken for President Johnson in 1966 by Edward M. Korry, Ambassador to Ethiopia.[12] In principle the countries marked out for favored status have been chosen on the basis of such criteria as their stability, prospects for growth, ability to help themselves by making effective use of aid and their own resources, and readiness to play a constructive role in regional affairs. The working reality, however, has often deviated from these principles under the pressure of international politics and of American interests and relationships.

The major recipients of American economic assistance from AID and its predecessor agencies, cumulatively from April 3, 1948 to June 30, 1965, and from the Food for Peace Program (Public Law 480), as well as the aid received in fiscal year 1965, are shown in Table 3 (000,000 omitted).[13]

TABLE 3 • *MAJOR AFRICAN RECIPIENTS OF U.S. AID*

Country	AID and predecessor agencies 1948-1965			FY 1965	Food for Peace Cumulative FY 1946-1965
	Loans	*Grants*	*Total*	*Total*	
Morocco	$270.1	$ 19.4	$289.5	$10.8	$192.1
Tunisia	118.2	110.2	228.4	17.8	213.0
Libya	7.1	130.6	137.7	*	35.3
Congo	15.0	192.9	207.9	15.8	90.9
Nigeria	57.6	79.2	136.8	25.7	2.2
Ethiopia	36.5	68.2	104.7	7.9	14.7
Liberia	48.3	55.3	103.6	15.2	10.5
Ghana	82.0	9.0	91.0	1.0	6.5
Sudan	15.8	55.3	71.1	2.7	18.4

* Less than $50,000

[12] See *The New York Times*, Sept. 4, 1966.

[13] See *Proposed Economic Assistance Programs FY 1967: Summary Presentation to the Congress*, prepared by the Agency for International Development (Washington: Govt. Printing Office, 1966), pp. 224-25, 229. The principal Export-Import Bank long-term loans for the period FY 1946-1965 were: South Africa $152,800,000; Liberia $88,700,000; Ghana $65,000,000; and UAR (Egypt) $47,800,000.

The complexities involved are illustrated by the fact that over two-thirds of the $150 million of AID loans and grants made to the whole of Africa (except the UAR, officially placed for these purposes in the Near East) in fiscal year 1965 went to seven countries in descending order: Nigeria, Tunisia, Congo, Liberia, Guinea, Morocco, and Ethiopia. In this list only Nigeria and Tunisia fell clearly within the officially stated criteria, and exceptional grounds had to be found for the inclusion of the remainder.

Following its independence, Nigeria was singled out by the American aid authorities as their favorite client in sub-Saharan Africa, although danger signals were increasingly evident in the last two or three years prior to the military take-over of January, 1966. Much the most populous African state, its moderation, its apparent ability to manage a democratic system, its economic planning which accepted private enterprise, and its neutralism benevolent to the West, all were congenial to the United States. On such grounds President Johnson in his message to Congress on foreign aid of January 14, 1965, named Nigeria as the only African state in the select company of seven countries which received 64 per cent of American development assistance because of their effective programs of self-help and ability to make good use of aid. The aid supplied by the United Kingdom, the International Bank and its affiliates, and other free world donors has come to nearly three times the American contribution.[14]

The broad sweep of activities covered by the American aid program in Nigeria indicates the diversity of American operations in Africa. The major capital assistance project, but one in which the American share is small, is the Niger Dam which should more than double the supply of electric power in the country. Agriculture, fishing, industry, tele-communications, roads, and water supply are among the many aspects of Nigerian life with which American aid has concerned itself. In the sphere of education the United States has played an important role, assisting, for example, in the training of teachers and technicians and the building up of both secondary and university education.

The most recent addition to the list of the favored few was the Congo, all too obviously not because of its strength and stability nor even because of its rich natural resources, but because of the threat that it might disintegrate and fall into Communist hands, as well as the fear that its internal conflicts might continue to embroil other African states. The effect of a crisis situation involving the Communists is indicated by the fact that although the Congo did not emerge as an American aid recipient

[14] *Proposed Mutual Defense and Development Programs FY 1966*, p. 137. See also *Programme for Progress: The Story of United States Co-operation with Nigeria's Development Plan* (published for the Agency for International Development by the United States Information Service, 1963). Arnold Rivkin has contended that if all American sources of aid are taken into account, Nigeria, despite being one of the favored states, has in fact received less assistance from the United States than several other countries which do not measure up to the "Kennedy economic development criteria" and which, in the cases of Guinea, Ghana, Mali, Algeria, and the UAR, are both politically suspect and unimpressive in economic performance. ("Lost Goals in Africa," *Foreign Affairs*, XLIV, No. 1, October, 1965, p. 125.)

until 1960, it had by June 30, 1965, been allocated more American aid—
primarily in the form of grants—than any other sub-Saharan African
country, and this apart from the American funds which flowed through
the UN and other international channels. The United States has also
encouraged the large Belgian program of financial aid and the provision
of different categories of skilled manpower. With diplomatic understate-
ment, however, the AID presentation to Congress of its program for
fiscal year 1966 commented that "Prospects for achieving complete stability in 1965 are not bright." [15]

Liberia's relatively high place on the American aid program derived
primarily from the old-established relationship between the two countries, although it was also stated, perhaps with a greater measure of hope
than of firm expectation, that Liberia was beginning to attack its larger
development problems. The American assistance program has aimed at
helping the country achieve needed institutional changes and carry out
basic reforms in public administration and budgetary policies.

In the case of Guinea the major factor was presumably the desire to
do whatever could be done to assist in keeping the country from drift-
ing into the Communist camp as it tended strongly to do after the breach
with France in 1958. Disaffection on the part of Sékou Touré with his
Communist entanglements encouraged the United States to join in trying to salvage what could be salvaged from the downward spiral which
threatened the Guinean economy. A prime consideration in relation to
Ethiopia was undoubtedly the American communications facility but the
country was also viewed as being an increasingly influential advocate for
stability and moderation in Africa, particularly as it became a focal point
for organizations embracing the entire African continent.

Principally in connection with the Volta Dam scheme, Ghana received
sizeable loans in 1961 and 1963 from the United States acting in conjunction with other countries and international agencies. In view of its inability to set its economic house in order, however, and its often vehemently
hostile attitude toward the United States, it increasingly fell into a disfavor from which the military coup of February, 1966, which ousted
President Nkrumah, rescued it.

In its *Proposed Economic Assistance Programs* for FY 1967, AID provided for aid for 33 African countries, aside from provision for the UAR
under the Near East heading. South Africa had always been out because
of its prosperity and more recently also because of the ill fame of
apartheid; Libya was dropped because of the size of its new-found oil
revenues; and Congo-Brazzaville was eliminated as a result of the leftward swing following the ouster of President Fulbert Youlou in December, 1963. The five African countries on which attention was focused for
1967 were the Congo, Nigeria, Ethiopia, Morocco, and Tunisia. Very
limited programs were proposed for the rest of the ex-French and Belgian
countries which receive substantial aid and trade benefits from the former
metropoles and the European Economic Community. The unreadiness
particularly of France to release its former colonies from its economic

[15] *Proposed Mutual Defense and Development Programs FY 1966*, p. 128.

sphere—or, in a different version, to force them out on their own in the cold world—has also impaired the ability to secure the African regional cooperation which Washington has set as one of the goals of its aid policy. The American intention has been to consolidate its aid in order to achieve a more substantial impact, and it has made some real headway; but it would be idle to ignore how irresistibly tempting it has been, and must continue to be, to distribute some morsels everywhere and in every category of need. The limitations imposed by Congress in the Foreign Assistance Act of 1966 on the over-all number of states to which aid can be furnished forced a reconsideration of the extent of the programs for Africa.

Challenging the customary lament that Africa has been the Cinderella of aid recipients, Secretary of State Rusk asserted in 1964 that:

> On a per capita basis, Africans get a larger share of the combined economic assistance of the United States and Europe than any other area of the world. In fact, Africa's per capita share is almost double the world average.[16]

In recent years the United States has contributed somewhere between a third and a quarter of the total assistance made available to Africa, including the increasing commitments of the Communist countries. France and Great Britain, with the former as the larger donor, have been the major sources of aid for Africa, and the European Economic Community has also made substantial contributions to the African states associated with it. As for the Communist powers, AID reported in March, 1965 that in contrast to a decline in total free-world aid from $1.7 billion to $1.2 billion between 1962 and 1964, Communist aid offers rose from about $200 million in fiscal year 1962 to $400 million in fiscal year 1964 with major increases coming from China.[17]

To attempt to find any permanent and universal answers to the host of questions which foreign aid raises soon becomes an exercise in doctrinaire logic which political necessities and pressures are sure to sweep away. It is a not irrelevant reflection that the United States is damned if it does and damned if it doesn't. If its aid programs are small or nonexistent, it is obviously failing to live up to its clear duty to help the impoverished and underdeveloped. If the programs are large, it is accused by its ex-colonial allies of trying to elbow them out; and by the leftwing, of neo-colonialism. All that is inescapably evident is that Africa's needs are immense and will be with us far into the future, although the ability of African countries to make effective use of massive

---

[16] Dean Rusk, "Freedom and Development," *Department of State Bulletin*, LI, No. 1320 (October 12, 1964), p. 500.

[17] *Proposed Mutual Defense and Development Programs FY 1966*, p. 122. As calculated by the Organization for Economic Co-operation and Development, the official contributions to less developed countries, including contributions to multilateral agencies, of France came to $975,000,000 in 1962 and $863,000,000 in 1963 while the British contributions in the same years were $421,000,000 and $414,000,000. A very large proportion of the French figure went to African countries formerly under French rule. *The Flow of Financial Resources to Less-Developed Countries, 1956-1963* (Paris: Organisation for Economic Co-operation and Development, 1964), p. 22.

injections of foreign aid must be constantly re-examined. To meet those needs the fullest possible collaboration of all potential donor countries is obviously to be sought, but the price of winning their collaboration is too high if the United States must be prepared to play a role secondary to that of the ex-colonial powers. As American relations with Africa evolve, it is essential that America both have, and make it apparent that it has, an independent policy toward African countries and not one contingent upon its relations with the former colonial metropoles.

The African countries as well as the rest of their underdeveloped colleagues find profoundly unsatisfactory the general international economic system of which the assistance programs, however desirable they may be in themselves, are a part. The slogan "trade not aid" embraces a substantial part of the problem but by no means all of it, in view of the tendency toward worsening terms of trade for raw material suppliers,[18] and the continued concentration of so many countries on one or two crops or minerals as their principal source of foreign exchange. Instead of being able to take an equal place in the world economy, the underdeveloped countries are still distressingly reliant on the markets, capital, and benevolence of the advanced and well-to-do. They are recipients of what is portrayed as charity rather than being able to pay their own way, but even as charity patients they are falling further behind, rather than gaining on the advanced peoples. One of the most serious issues, the full effects of which are still to be felt, is that the underdeveloped are piling up foreign debts, the payment of which will present immense difficulties. Basically of far greater importance than the improvement of measures of economic assistance is the need to rethink and reorient the whole system of international economy which leaves the newly independent in fact so vulnerable and so dependent.

PEACE CORPS

The most distinctive contribution which the United States has made to the independent countries of Africa as well as to other parts of the so-called Third World, made up of the developing countries, is the creation of the Peace Corps, a conception which has since been copied by a number of other states. In essence, what is involved is an instrumentality which taps the idealism, the altruism, the restlessness, and the adventurousness primarily of young men and women, but with no fixed barriers of age, and makes them available to underdeveloped peoples around the globe. The Peace Corps volunteers themselves are offered a rewarding, challenging, and often hazardous experience of serving others and of living intimately with distant peoples, which in some respects closely resembles the missionary experience. The people among whom they

[18] Andrew Kamarck contended that as a result of a deterioration in the terms of trade, "in the main, on the average, Africa is having to pay prices that are perhaps 10 per cent higher today than they were in 1960, while the prices of the commodities they sell decreased year by year until in 1962, they were 15 per cent below the average of 1955-57." ("Recent Growth in Africa," *Africa in Motion*, ed. Thorsten Sellin. *The Annals of the American Academy of Political and Social Sciences*, July, 1964, p. 53.)

serve are by no means the only gainers: the life of the volunteers is enriched, and perhaps the greatest benefit of all is to the American society as a whole which profits immensely from the existence of thousands of returned volunteers who bring not only a firsthand knowledge of another land but often also a warm enthusiasm for it and its inhabitants.[19]

The Peace Corps was inevitably a gamble, and it has had its ups and downs, but in the large it has been successful beyond reasonable expectation. To turn so many Americans loose in Africa, normally with only some three months training and often living off by themselves in remote parts of the country to which they were sent is to invite trouble of many different kinds. The amazing thing is how relatively slight and infrequent it has been and how cordially the Americans have been welcomed. The overdramatized incident of early Peace Corps days in Nigeria when a volunteer's postcard critical of some of Nigeria's ways was intercepted on the way home and publicized in the country was a warning of some of the difficulties which were to be expected, but neither embroilment with the host country nor the cracking up of volunteers due to culture shock or more material ailments has been a significant feature of the Peace Corps venture.

Africa has bulked large in Peace Corps operations, coming in a close second after Latin America and far ahead of the two other major categories of the Far East and the Near East and South Asia. The relative standing of these regions as of June 30, 1965 is shown in Table 4.

TABLE 4 • *PEACE CORPS VOLUNTEERS BY WORLD REGIONS, 1965*

Region	In training	Overseas
Latin America	1690	3214
Near East and South Asia	863	1285
Far East	785	847
Africa	1136	3010

Source: Peace Corps, 4th Annual Report (Washington: Peace Corps, 1965), pp. 7-12.

The greatest measure of the success which the Peace Corps has achieved is the repeated request by a number of countries for an increase in the number of Peace Corps workers, who are, of course, not sent into any country save by official invitation. In Africa both the number of host countries and the number of volunteers in the field has increased spectacularly. On June 30, 1962, only 232 members of the Peace Corps were working in four countries; two years later this figure had risen to 2,093 in fourteen countries; and on June 30, 1965, the total had risen to 3,010 volunteers in seventeen countries. The largest number and the most striking increase occurred in Nigeria which climbed from 109 volunteers in 1962 to 634 in 1965, followed by Ethiopia with 278 Peace Corps workers in 1963 and 565 in 1965. Almost all the former British territories were involved in the operations of the Peace Corps but only half a dozen of the fifteen states formerly attached to France.

[19] See *Citizen in a Time of Change: The Returned Peace Corps Volunteer*, Report of the Conference, Washington, D.C., March 5-7, 1965.

By far the most important role of the Peace Corps in Africa has been in the sphere of education, since 80 per cent of the volunteers are serving as teachers. For the most part they are engaged in secondary-school teaching, which is still generally the most grievous bottleneck in the educational system, but they function at many other points in the different educational systems as well. Many are engaged in teaching English, but their range covers virtually the entire gamut of academic subjects.

In addition to teaching, Peace Corps volunteers have served in many other capacities in Africa. In several countries community development workers have sought to assist local communities in meeting their own needs through the building of schools and roads, wells and latrines. Agriculture, fisheries, and home economics have occupied other Peace Corps volunteers; and in the field of health, medical teams have included doctors, dentists, nurses, and technicians. In the realm of public works, "Architects, engineers, surveyors, general laborers, and machine and motor repairmen are helping to build roads and highways, dams, water supply systems, schools, clinics, libraries, housing and other needed structures." [20]

These are, in a sense, the bare bones of the Peace Corps project, but it is probable that the long-run effect of the Peace Corps is the human contacts which it establishes on both sides of the ocean, rather than the teaching which it accomplishes, the health which it safeguards, or the roads it builds. It is, among many other things, of marked importance that Africans should come to know Americans other than embassy personnel, businessmen, or tourists congregated primarily in the urban centers. Through the Peace Corps, Africans have been brought in contact with Americans living simple lives in African surroundings and doing comprehensible jobs in concert with Africans.

To counterbalance what may seem too idyllic a picture, the hostile verdict of ex-President Nkrumah. who undoubtedly reflected the suspicions of many Africans, should be cited. In his view the Peace Corps was only one phase of "a huge ideological plan for invading the so-called Third World," which the United States had been developing since 1961. Headed by a millionaire, Sargent Shriver, Jr., who was an intimate friend of the former CIA chief, Allen Dulles, the Peace Corps was seen as closely linked to the CIA, having been brought in to cover the ideological arena when Moral Re-Armament began to lose its influence. Since it started in 1961, according to Nkrumah,

> members of the Peace Corps have been exposed and expelled from many African, Middle Eastern, and Asian countries for acts of subversion or prejudice. Indonesia, Tanzania, the Philippines, and even pro-West countries like Turkey and Iran, have complained of its activities. [21]

[20] *Peace Corps in Africa* (brochure issued in 1965 by the Peace Corps, Washington), p. 11.
[21] Kwame Nkrumah, *Neo-Colonialism, The Last Stage of Imperialism* (London: Nelson, 1965), pp. 247-49. Moral Re-Armament is an evangelistic religious movement, also known as the Oxford Group, founded early in the present century by Frank N. D. Buchman as the means to achieve both world and domestic peace and prosperity.

In the light of this imaginatively colorful account, the extraordinary feature is that the demand for Peace Corps volunteers has constantly multiplied, and, even more striking, ten days after the publication of the book in which these charges were made, Nkrumah's Ministry of Education requested 91 mathematics and science teachers to replace the 48 volunteers whose term was to expire in the following July. On June 30, 1965, there were 110 Peace Corps members serving in Ghana. Since Ghana pays nearly $2,000 a year for each volunteer, it seems a reasonable presumption that when they are no longer needed, or are feared more than they are needed, they will no longer be requested. The most grievous blow suffered by the Peace Corps came in November, 1966, through no fault of its own. Holding the United States partly responsible for Ghana's forcible removal of the Guinean Foreign Minister and other Guineans from a Pan-American plane in Accra, on their way to an OAU summit meeting, Sékou Touré demanded immediate withdrawal of all Peace Corps personnel from Guinea.

Although others shared in devising the original conception of the Peace Corps, it was a project particularly close to the heart of President Kennedy, whose interest in Africa was strong. Nowhere has the Peace Corps played a more vital role or scored a larger success than in the African countries, whose needs and ability to absorb this type of assistance are immense. The enthusiasm of the men and women drawn into the Peace Corps has been encouraged to find full expression in the type of structure which was developed in the first years of its existence. As Arthur M. Schlesinger, Jr. has put it,

> It was no accident that the organization which best expressed the distinctive spirit of the New Frontier—the Peace Corps—was almost the only one established as an emergency agency and carefully preserved from the embrace of the bureaucracy.[22]

It remains to be seen what will become of it as it settles down into more routine administrative procedures.

AFRICAN EDUCATION

American involvement in African education has deep roots. Africans and people of African descent on both sides of the ocean have long maintained contacts of many different kinds with each other, and American missionary enterprises, both black and white, have made impressive contributions to African education. The last few years have witnessed an impressive expansion of the American concern, but earlier decades produced many notable results, including the ground-breaking reports of the African Education Commissions established under the Phelps-Stokes Fund to survey African education in the early 1920's. More recently, through official as well as private channels, the United States has helped to plan, to man, and to finance a number of educational institutions, and close ties have been established between certain American

[22] *A Thousand Days* (Boston: Houghton, 1965), p. 683.

and African universities on a cooperative basis. Thus, the University of Nigeria at Nsukka, close to the heart of former President Azikiwe of Nigeria who was the main mover in its creation, has been intimately related to Michigan State University. The Peace Corps and several privately organized and financed programs have sought to fill some of Africa's needs for qualified teachers to meet the insatiable popular demand for schooling.

Long before Ghana's independence started the landslide which has swept away most of Africa's colonialism, American schools, colleges, and universities had played a significant role in the education of African students. In the nineteenth and earlier twentieth centuries only a handful of Africans found their way to school in this country, usually under religious auspices. Since the mid-1950's a constantly increasing stream of African students, for the most part supported by American private, Foundation, and official funds, has been coming to the United States primarily to round out their higher education. The numbers of those who come to the United States, although far from negligible, are still much smaller than those who go to Great Britain or France, usually from their former colonies. In recent years American students and scholars have also increasingly made their way to Africa, sometimes dismaying officials and their African colleagues by their numbers and the researches they pursue, but their total is slight compared to the Africans coming to the United States.

The bare figures of African students in this country as they have grown over the last decade are impressive enough in themselves. Of the total number of 34,232 foreign students in the United States in 1954-1955, the Africans from the entire continent came to 1,234, or 3.6 per cent, while a decade later, in 1964-1965, the African contingent had mounted to 6,865 of a total of 82,045, or 8.4 per cent.[23] For six consecutive years, from 1958-1959 to 1964-1965, the percentage increase of students coming from Africa was greater than that for any other geographical area, the overwhelming majority coming from the English-speaking territories, with no more than a handful from the French or Portuguese-speaking areas. In 1954-1955 only six countries sent more than twenty-five students: Egypt 351, Nigeria 268, Liberia 188, South Africa 157, Gold Coast 81, Sierra Leone 27. In 1964-1965, ten African states had more than 200 students in the United States:

Nigeria	1,382	Tanzania	305
UAR	1,279	Ghana	282
Kenya	774	Ethiopia	266
South Africa	390	Uganda	223
Liberia	315	Rhodesia	203

Among the French-speaking countries, Guinea's breach with France pushed it into the lead with 99 students, followed by the Congo with 94.

African students have come to the United States under many dif-

---

[23] These and the immediately following statistics are drawn from the Institute of International Education's annual publication *Open Doors*, for 1954-1955 and 1965.

ferent auspices. A substantial number have come on their own or through projects which did not reach far beyond getting them started here,[24] but a large proportion of those who came in this fashion have run into serious financial or other difficulties. The best planned and executed of the programs to bring African students here is known as ASPAU—the African Scholarship Program of American Universities.[25] Under this program more than 200 American colleges and universities have banded together to supplement educational opportunities available in Africa by enabling qualified African students to study for the bachelor's degree. The program started in 1960 when 24 Nigerian students were enrolled in 19 American colleges. By 1967 ASPAU had brought 1,306 students from more than 30 African countries with Nigeria still far in the lead.

The three outstanding features of this program have been its selection processes, which have been unusually successful, its care in seeing to the orientation and placement of students in the United States, and its financing. The latter, which is intended to meet all legitimate expenses of the student from departure from his own country until his return there after securing his B.A. degree, is met from several sources: the student's own government, AID, American Foundations, and the academic institutions concerned which contribute the student's tuition and fees.

Any large-scale American involvement in African education immediately raises a host of problems. Should there be a present concentration on educating Africans in the United States or on building up African schools and universities, or how should resources be divided between the two? Should study in the United States be made available primarily to undergraduates or to graduate students, and how serious is the risk in either category of depriving African universities of their best students? What are the disciplines or courses of study which should be promoted, and how closely should they be geared to the development plans and ascertained needs of particular countries? These are questions which must be constantly reviewed as the situation changes in different countries and regions with an eye also to the weathervane of shifting political susceptibilities. As for disciplines, the trend has been toward increasing emphasis on engineering and the natural sciences, and a closer watch is being kept by African governments on fitting students to their manpower needs. On general grounds it seems clear that the expansion of African institutions of higher learning, which deserves full American support, should mean a curtailment of programs for bringing African undergraduates to this country and a concentration on graduate training, particularly on specialized programs not available at home. A further problem,

[24] The most dramatic event of this sort was the Kenya airlift of 1960 and 1961 which brought some hundreds of Kenyan and other East African students to the United States. See Tom Mboya, *Freedom and After* (London: Deutsch, 1963), Chapter 7.

[25] For an account of this program, see *African Students and Study Programs in the United States,* Report and Hearings of the Subcommittee on Africa, House Committee on Foreign Affairs, House Report No. 809, 89th Cong., 1st sess., August 18, 1965 (Washington: Govt. Printing Office), pp. 40-46, 56-64.

peculiar to the American scene, is presented by the Negro American who contrasts the benefits opened up to African students with the discrimination to which he has so often been subjected in the United States.

One sphere of American activity deserves special mention because it touches upon the highly sensitive area of white-dominated southern Africa. What is involved is the provision of educational facilities for the refugees from southern Africa who have been increasingly moving into the neighboring independent African states, notably Tanzania, Zambia, and the Congo, and who are also wooed by the Communists. The two central needs to be met are the great desire of the refugees themselves for education and the ultimate need of their countries for men and women educated to shoulder the responsibilities which will, be it sooner or later, come their way. In Tanzania and Zambia the African-American Institute, in consultation with the governments of the two countries, has established schools giving a secondary education to southern African refugees as well as some students from the country in which the school is located. Since the prior education of many of the students has been spotty and interrupted, a pre-secondary program has also proved necessary to make up deficiencies and to teach English. The two schools are to have a combined capacity of some 550 students, and will offer instruction in administration as well as the standard program of studies preparing the way for college entry.

A higher level of instruction for southern African refugees is provided in the United States by the Special African Student Program established by the Department of State in 1961. Working in conjunction with the African-American Institute, the Department provides scholarships for students lacking the customary academic documents and with other substantive gaps in their education, including inadequate command of English, thus making them ineligible for the conventional scholarships. By arrangement with Lincoln and Rochester universities, African students who have been screened by American Foreign Service officers can be received at any time and are given special training to qualify them to start regular undergraduate careers. By the autumn of 1965, there had been 339 students enrolled in this program, whose annual intake is about 120 a year. As Assistant Secretary of State Williams put it:

> This program provides an attractive alternative to study in Communist countries. The education the students receive here will help prepare them to make a responsible, constructive contribution to the development of Africa and to provide intelligent and democratic leadership to their people.[26]

Collaboration between the United States and Africa in the broad sphere of education represents an adventure, well-equipped with hazards, which can be of great cultural, social, and political consequence. Although the balance is already being somewhat redressed, in the early

[26] From statement by G. Mennen Williams before the Senate Judiciary Committee's Subcommittee on Refugees and Escapees, Washington, January 21, 1965.

phases the benefits must on the whole flow from America to Africa, since Africa has still so long a road to travel in moving toward full-scale entry into the modern world. Already, however, many Americans are coming to know Africa at first hand, and Africans are bringing to the United States a new and fresh sense of their swiftly changing continent.

MISSIONARIES

One of the most significant and continuing points of contact between the United States and Africa has been American missionary activity, which has increased substantially in recent decades. In 1959 it was reported that missionaries were the most numerous of any category of American citizens resident in Africa.[27]

In addition to their directly religious work, the missions have made major contributions in the sphere of health and medicine and most notably in education. In many instances they were not only the most immediate and intimate links between the West and the Africans of the bush, but also did pioneering work in opening to the outside world a knowledge of African languages and in reducing these languages to written form, if only for the primary purpose of making access to the Gospels possible. More recently it has been necessary for the missions to turn their attention increasingly from the countryside and hinterland to the grievous problems of the urban centers where the villagers crowd into the misery of the slums.

As far as Americans are concerned, Africa has been an area open primarily to the Protestant churches, since Catholic missionary activity has been chiefly manned and directed from Europe. Firm statistics as to American mission operations are difficult to come by, but in 1961 it was authoritatively estimated that of 26,390 American Protestant missionaries serving overseas about one-third, or nearly 8,800, were serving in Africa, almost all south of the Sahara, as compared with less than 3,000 in 1925 and some 6,800 in 1956.[28] Nigeria was stated to have attracted well over 1,200 American Protestant missionaries, the largest contingent in any African country, followed by the Congo which also had over 1,200 although many left the country in the turmoil which followed independence. In contrast, the number of American Catholic missionaries in Africa on January 1, 1964, was reported to be 1,016 or 12 per cent of the

[27] *United States Foreign Policy, Africa*, A Study Prepared at the Request of the Committee on Foreign Relations, United States Senate by Program of African Studies, Northwestern University, No. 4 (October 23, 1959) Washington: Govt. Printing Office, 1959, p. 43.

[28] For the statistics on Protestant missionaries, see *Activities of Private United States Organizations in Africa*, Hearings before the Subcommittee on Africa of the Committee on Foreign Affairs, House of Representatives, 87th Cong., 1st sess. (Washington: Govt. Printing Office, 1961), p. 133. A later report estimated that in 1963, American Protestant missionary personnel in Africa came to 6,827; and United States and Canadian mission expenditures in Africa amounted to $31,231,068 (R. D. Gatewood, *Some American Protestant Contributions to the Welfare of African Countries in 1963*. New York: National Council of the Churches of Christ in the USA, December, 1964, p. viii.)

global total, representing an increase of 125 since 1960. The great bulk of the Catholic missionaries have gone to the English-speaking countries of Africa. Tanganyika and Ghana led the list in 1964 with 245 and 114 respectively.[29]

Politically the missions have been attacked from opposite sides, accused both of being the agents of colonialism, treating their wards with paternalistic superiority, and of having a large share of responsibility for stirring up nationalist disaffection. Both charges are presumably justified. On the nationalist score, it was one of the noteworthy features of the early phases of the revolt which broke out in northern Angola in 1961 that the Portuguese authorities promptly took action to curb the work of American Protestant missionaries in the country. Although the churches have often been charged with not living up to their responsibilities, Christian doctrine is in many ways implicitly or explicitly incompatible with the maintenance of the kind of relationships characteristic of colonialism. This appeared unmistakably in a declaration, "American Christian Responsibility toward Africa," issued in 1956 by the National Council of the Churches of Christ in the United States. In its broadest statement of policy this document held that while the United States has no direct political stake in Africa, it cannot disassociate itself from major concern for its peoples.

> Three hundred years of the slave trade not only transplanted millions of Africa's sons and daughters to America, but also created the myth of Negro inferiority from which we are still struggling to get free. The insatiable demand of our Western economy for minerals and other raw materials has drawn millions of Africans into mines and plantations, often under conditions which destroy family life and social cohesion. The West has thrust itself upon Africa; we cannot remain indifferent to the consequences.[30]

More specifically, the Council called for an end of all political and social patterns involving the subjection of one racial or cultural group to another. "We believe," the statement affirmed, "that peace, stability, and progress will only be assured when race ceases to be a criterion of political, social, or economic status." The Council shied off from any forthright demand for political advance, warning that African political development should not be seen as itself a panacea and that nationalism might be a divisive rather than a unifying force. Its emphasis was laid on the utopian hope of the growth of a multiracial society in which all would contribute to a common nationhood.

That the churches and missionaries have often fallen short of their professed aims is also clear on the record. A discriminatory racist attitude

[29] *U.S. Catholic Missionary Personnel Overseas, January 1, 1964* (Washington: Mission Secretariat, August, 1964), pp. v, vi, xi. Cameroun was also listed as having 11 American Catholic missionaries, but these were probably resident in what used to be the British rather than the French section of the country.

[30] This document was drawn up by the Africa Committee of the Council's Division of Foreign Missions. For the text, see the congressional report, *Activities of Private United States Organizations in Africa*, pp. 134-39.

has been far from unknown in missionary circles, and the temptation to look down upon and condemn all Africa's "heathen" and "primitive" ways and beliefs has often proved irresistible. Despite recognition that speedy moves must be made to transfer control to Africans, the Africa Committee responsible for drawing up the 1956 statement said the following year that in some cases the investment of an African church with autonomy had been more apparent than real as missionaries proved "unwilling or unable to divest themselves of long-established habits of taking the lead." [31]

In many instances African churches have broken away from their alien sponsorship to manage their own affairs, or Christian converts have established churches of their own, often more closely adapted to the African tradition and outlook than white missionaries were prepared to accept. Occasionally also American sects and religious movements have spread to Africa with dramatic results, as, for example, in the case of the Watchtower, known in the Congo as the Kitawala movement, suppressed by the Belgian authorities. An earlier episode which also had its American religious connections was the Nyasaland rising of 1915 in which John Chilembwe, who had spent some time in the United States, played a leading role.[32]

However vehement and derogatory the criticisms which have been directed at them, and they have been many, the Christian missions have played a great role and still have much to contribute. As the African peoples take over the management of their own affairs, all phases of missionary activity must, however, be re-examined, and Africanization must become, as it already has in many instances, a first order of business. In all spheres, but perhaps most notably in education, the control by African governments is greatly intensified where missionary educational enterprises are not wholly supplanted by a governmental educational system. With the progress of Africanization the role of the alien missionary tends to be more and more restricted. Nor can it be a matter which Christian churches contemplate with equanimity that Islam appears to have shown an ability to move ahead in Africa more swiftly than Christianity, perhaps because of its greater readiness to adapt itself to African ways and attitudes.

[31] Africa Committee, *Advance in Africa* (New York: Division of Foreign Missions, NCCC, 1957), p. 18. Although elementary schools accounted for the great bulk of the institutions receiving foreign assistance, their teaching staff was almost wholly African, while 90 per cent of the non-African teachers were in secondary schools or more advanced institutions. The African churches themselves are now almost everywhere responsible for the management of church-related schools. (Gatewood, *Some American Protestant Contributions to the Welfare of African Countries in 1963*, p. 147.)

[32] Robert I. Rotberg, *The Rise of Nationalism in Central Africa, The Making of Malawi and Zambia 1873-1964* (Cambridge, Mass.: Harvard University, 1965), pp. 76 ff. He also deals with the Watchtower movement in Central Africa, pp. 136 ff. For more information on Chilembwe, see George Shepperson and Thomas Price, *Independent African* (Edinburgh, 1958).

5

The Negro American

The most vital and unique concern of the United States with Africa derives from the existence of that 10 per cent of the American population which in whole or in part traces its ancestry to Africa. Because the Negro American is still deeply involved in the processes of achieving his equal place, and hence his proper significance, in the American society, he has not yet attained the full potential of his ability to influence African-American relations. It may be taken for granted that in the coming years both his interest in Africa and his power to do something about it will sharply increase.

The massive attack on racialism in the United States is by no means only a domestic matter in either its origins or its consequences. What has been happening in Africa and in the nonwhite world in general is forcing far more basic changes in racial attitudes and relationships than can be adequately assessed while the world is still caught up in a series of revolutions of which the overturn of colonialism is only one phase. Difficult as it may be to form a precise estimate, it is, however, beyond question that the emergence of the galaxy of independent African states has had profound effects on the American domestic scene and on the Negro view of Africa. As America has contributed in a variety of ways to the rise of the new Africa, so the new Africa, in return, has greatly influenced the position and outlook of the Negro American.

The relationship of the Negro American to Africa has been, and in good part continues to be, ambiguous, hesitant, and divided. To a tragic extent the Negro has denied the African phase of his heritage by accepting the low opinion of Africa and Africans characteristic of the white-dominated society in which he lives. The peoples of Africa were habitually presented as primitive pagans—"natives" in the derogatory sense of the term—with the stock comic strip depicting them as dancing about the boiling pot in which the missionary or trader was about to vanish. The African, it was asserted, had no history or distinctive culture of his own and was properly subordinate to the colonial regimes which were bringing civilization to him. For the white man the maintenance of basic propositions such as these was an essential conditon for the justification of slavery and the slave trade, colonialism, and segregation and discrimination, whether of the American or the South African variety.

Many among the Negroes came to accept the corollary proposition that black was a color which stood at the bottom of the scale of values while white represented all that was good and desirable. James Baldwin has said that Negroes in the United States are taught to despise themselves from the moment they open their eyes: "This world is white and they are black. White people hold the power, which means that they are superior to blacks (intrinsically, that is: God decreed it so). . . ."[1] Against a background such as this, African origin was not something in which the Negro was likely to take pride unless he was prepared to strike out vigorously against the main currents of the society. On the contrary, it was easy and consoling to swing to the opinion that the Negro's share in the American heritage endowed him with superiority to the African "natives," much as the Americo-Liberians, descended from slaves returned to Africa, asserted their superiority over the Africans of the bush.

Very different alternative strands have also always been present. The other side of the coin is represented by the many Negroes in the United States, and in the West Indies as well, who over the centuries have retained an identification with Africa, or, alienated from the white man's world, have reached out to create and cement such ties. At a number of times the sense that the Negro had no proper place in America and that Africa was his homeland has led to movements on a large or small scale looking to a return to their continent of the descendants of those whom the slavers had transported across the Atlantic. One such movement, backed in part by whites who wanted to rid the United States of the dangerous presence of freed slaves, led to the creation of Liberia in the first half of the nineteenth century as a place of settlement for Negroes shipped back across the Atlantic. A far more flamboyant movement, but one which produced no result in African resettlement, was the drive in the 1920's by Marcus Garvey, a West Indian who made Harlem his headquarters, to reverse the established order of things by seeing blackness as a matter not of shame but of pride, by securing the rights of the Negro peoples of the world, and by undertaking a mass return of Negroes to Africa. The imperial ambitions with which he endowed himself, his Universal Negro Improvement Association, and such subsidiary enterprises as his Black Star Line, were ultimately self-defeating, but he brought a new

[1] James Baldwin, *The Fire Next Time* (New York: Dell, 1964), p. 40.

dynamism and a new dimension to the Negro American community. Indeed, ex-President Nkrumah of Ghana has insisted, after naming Hegel, Marx, Engels, Lenin, and Mazzini, that "of all the literature that I studied, the book that did more than any other to fire my enthusiasm was *The Philosophy and Opinions of Marcus Garvey.*" [2]

In a far quieter fashion, with little or no acquaintance by the rest of the American community with what was going on, intercourse between Africa and Negro Americans was maintained by a variety of groups in this country, for the most part with strong religious affiliations. Through such groups Negro missionaries and others were sent to Africa, and they built up contacts with Africans which the colonial authorities were increasingly inclined to frown upon, on the correct assumption that, whatever the original intent, subversive influences were directly or indirectly at work. Negro church and educational bodies also reversed the flow, bringing to the United States Africans who later returned to their own countries to set new forces in motion. Among other things, such contacts served to stimulate the creation of separatist African churches which ran their own affairs and demonstrated the ability of Africans to get out from under white control. Both white and Negro scholars in the United States carried on research in African history, attempting to fill the void which furnished one of the excuses for white supremacy. The pre-eminent Negro American leader of the first decades of the present century, W.E.B. Du Bois, was involved throughout his life not only in dealing with the problems of race and color at home and throughout the world as well, but also in shaping the ideology of pan-Africanism and organizing a series of pan-African conferences, starting in 1919. In 1963 he died at the age of 95 in Ghana, where he had become a citizen and was directing the preparation of an *Encyclopedia Africana.*

An outstanding student of the relations between Negro Americans and Africa has concluded that:

> Negro Americans, in a complicated Atlantic triangle of influences, have played a considerable part ideologically in the emergence of African nationalism: in conceptualization, evocation of attitudes, and through the provision of the raw material of history. If, today, the new African nations may be said to be of more value to Negro America than Negro America to them, this should not be allowed to conceal the historical role of the coloured American in their emergence. [3]

Even despite the recent rise of Africa to front-page headlines, it is presumably still the fact that the bulk of the Negro American community is indifferent to Africa if only because of lack of knowledge of the continent and its peoples, and this indifference also extends to many better-educated Negroes who take only a minimal interest in the continent or prefer to turn away from it. Obviously, Negro Americans have no set at-

[2] Kwame Nkrumah, *Ghana, The Autobiography of Kwame Nkrumah* (New York: Nelson, 1957), p. 45.

[3] George Shepperson, "Notes on Negro American Influences on the Emergence of African Nationalism," in *Independent Black Africa,* ed. William John Hanna (Chicago: Rand McNally, 1964), pp. 192-207.

titude to Africa imposed upon them by the fact that some or all of their ancestors came from some unknown part of it in the remote past. By an act of will they may choose to associate themselves with Africa in any degree from full identification to a distant and speculative interest; or they may seek full and equal absorption into the American people; or demand some sort of recognition as a distinct nationality within the United States, including the allocation of a separate national territory. On the face of it, the Negro Americans have no more reason to identify themselves with Africa than have other Americans to make much of their pre-American heritage. The very different positions which have been taken by Jewish Americans toward Zionism and Israel are immediately illustrative of the ways in which Negroes may divide in their view of Africa. The one situation which would be likely to promote an identification with Africa on a large scale would arise if the American society proved unable to accomplish a satisfactory integration of the Negro. In that event the Negro would surely seek some other solution, and an identification with Africa as either a spiritual or an actual homeland is one of the paths which would be open to him, but a mass migration of Negro Americans is highly improbable. It is more likely that Africa would come to be seen as a rallying point for Negro group identity and as providing a psychological cloak of protection in the Diaspora, including a distinctive heritage of culture and history.[4] Whatever the ambivalence and ambiguities of the position of some Negro Americans, the main stream of contemporary history makes unmistakable the intimate relation between the emergence of the new African and Asian countries and the great drive for civil rights in the United States. Harold R. Isaacs has put the matter succinctly:

> The downfall of the white-supremacy system in the rest of the world made its survival in the United States suddenly and painfully conspicuous. It became our most exposed feature and in the swift unfolding of the world's affairs, our most vulnerable weakness . . . when hundreds of millions of people all around the world looked in our direction it seemed to be all they could see.[5]

A basic change in public morality, a global shift in attitudes, has in one circumstance expressed itself in the emergence of Asian and African states and in another in an attack upon the color bar. The "climate of rising expectations" which has been so central a theme in the developing countries could not be expected to leave untouched the underprivileged in the highly developed United States. The rise to prominence of African states and leaders and their role in the UN and elsewhere on the world stage has given new heart to Negroes who have drawn the obvious moral that if freedom can come to men with dark skins in other continents, it must also come to those in America. A world to be made safe for democracy in

[4] See the unpublished paper by Adelaide Cromwell Hill, "How the American Negro Relates to Africa," prepared for the Second National Congress of the American Negro Leadership Conference on Africa, 1964.
[5] Harold R. Isaacs, *The New World of the Negro Americans* (New York: Viking, 1964).

World War I, to be rid of racism in World War II, and dedicated to human rights and fundamental freedoms after that war, is not one in which the color bar can tranquilly survive.

The rise of African countries to sovereignty had certain direct and important consequences for the United States.[6] Apart from the fundamental proposition that African states hold an imposing number of seats in the UN and must be reckoned with on the international scene, probably the most significant development was the appearance in the United States of unprecedentedly large numbers of African and Asian diplomats and their staffs and families, not to mention the influx of students and other nonwhite visitors. To quote a distinguished Negro American anthropologist, Elliott P. Skinner, appointed Ambassador to Upper Volta in 1966, "For the first time in its history, America found itself compelled by world events to deal with black men on the basis of full equality." [7]

The issue was an all too obvious one. Negro Americans were expected to live in segregated quarters, were subject to exclusion from many public places and facilities, and were supposed to know and keep their place. The African student and casual visitor, however much he may have resented it, might have had to accept such discrimination as the price of being in this country; but the representatives of sovereign African states, their colonial experience having made them extremely sensitive to any slight, were in no mood to be pushed around as inferior. To mention only a single repeated source of earlier trouble, African diplomats traveling between Washington and the UN in New York found themselves excluded from roadside restaurants in Maryland on the sole ground of their color. What made it all the more intolerable was that they were excluded not because they were Africans—if it were established that they were foreigners, they might have had easier access—but because it was assumed that they were Americans. In order to achieve respect for the African dignitary it was obviously necessary to achieve respect for all Americans as well. An intensive drive by the authorities in Washington to clean up the Maryland highway situtation was mandatory; but this touched only the fringes of a problem which everywhere, but particularly in Washington and New York, involved so many aspects of life: housing, education, restaurants, places of entertainment, and so on down the line.

The United States now had to live in a world of color, seek to make friends and influence people who were black and brown and yellow, and to live and do business with states which were predominantly nonwhite. In such a world it might be widely appreciated that the United States differed fundamentally from South Africa in that it was trying to end and not intensify apartheid, but it needed no Communists to broadcast everywhere the pictures and stories of Negro children excluded from school, of race riots, of police dogs leaping at Negro throats, and of the brutal treatment and indeed the murder of civil rights advocates, the assailants

[6] See Rupert Emerson and Martin Kilson, "The American Dilemma in a Changing World: The Rise of Africa and the Negro American," *Dædalus,* Fall, 1965, pp. 1055-84.
[7] Elliott P. Skinner, "African, Afro-American, White American: A Case of Pride and Prejudice," *Freedomways,* V, No. 3 (Summer, 1965), p. 386.

almost always getting off scot-free. Where at an earlier stage American racial difficulties were essentially a domestic problem, they now became a matter of headline international concern, gravely impairing the ability of the United States to secure the respect and support for its policies which it sought. The concern of Secretary of State Rusk was vigorously expressed at a meeting of leading Negroes in Washington which he had called to explore the problem of equality of opportunity in the Department of State.

> The biggest single burden that we carry on our backs in our foreign relations in the 1960's is the problem of racial discrimination here at home. There is just no question about it.
>
> We are dealing with forty or fifty new countries that have become independent since 1945, and we are living through a decade of readjustment of the relationships between Western Europe and the rest of the world—a decade when the white race and the non-white races have got to re-examine and readjust their traditional relationships.
>
> Our attitude on a question of this sort is of fundamental importance to the success of the foreign policy of the United States.[8]

On a succeeding day, Chief S.O. Adebo, Permanent Representative of Nigeria to the UN, spoke to the same conference of the internationalizing of the problem of color.

> I no longer think simply as a Nigerian; I no longer think simply as an African. I think more as a person of color. And the objective of all of us is to restore to the man of color, wherever he may be, whether in Nigeria, or in the United States, or in Moscow, or in Brazil, the dignity of a human being. That is why we are involved in the same struggle in Africa, here, and elsewhere.[9]

The appearance of African states, the re-evaluation of Africa's cultural and artistic contribution, and the rewriting of African history to restore the continent to a reputable place in man's development, all have had the effect of lending valuable support to the claim of the Negro American to be accepted as an equal member both of the American nation and the human race. It is, of course, also true that where things have gone wrong in Africa, as in the troubled Congo, the assassinations or attempted assassinations of leaders, the military coups, the widespread corruption or the mutinies in East Africa which required the calling in of British troops, the result, inevitably, is to confirm the opinions of those who, like Senator Ellender or the whites of South Africa and Rhodesia, believe that Negroes, whether in Africa or here, are incapable of managing their own affairs. The net effect of Africa's emergence, however, is unquestionably to strengthen the Negro's hand in winning a kind of status which was formerly denied him.

[8] Cited by John A. Davis in a paper, "The Employment of American Negroes in the Foreign Service of the United States," prepared for the American Negro Leadership Conference on Africa, held in Harriman, New York, November 23-25, 1962, p. 11.
[9] Extemporaneous speech to the American Negro Leadership Conference on Africa on September 29, 1964.

Of the steps taken in the United States to put an end to segregation only one will be mentioned because of its international implications: the drive to secure Negro participation in the American Foreign Service. The earlier state of affairs has been described in the following terms:

> In the old days before 1950 all Negroes, with the exception of one, were in the Foreign Service Staff Corps (the administrative and clerical support group) and all Negroes, without exception, served only in Africa, usually in Liberia or the Canary Islands. The principle of rotation from hardship posts to more pleasant posts did not apply to Negroes. The best estimates indicate that there were only about 25 Negroes in the Foreign Service Staff Corps and one in the Foreign Service Officer Corps before 1950.[10]

With varying degrees of enthusiasm and application, a concerted effort has been made since 1950 to enlist a larger number of Negroes in the Foreign Service and to secure the assignment of Negroes to ministerial or ambassadorial posts other than Monrovia. On both scores, a substantial advance has been achieved, although the Negro representation is still far below the proportion of Negroes in the American population. More Negroes with adequate qualifications can undoubtedly be drawn into the State Department and Foreign Service, but the hard core of the problem can be dealt with only by the elimination of race discrimination in the American society and the winning of educational equality with the whites for the Negroes.

Despite the pledges and efforts of a decade and a half, by 1964, of the total of 10,987 persons at a professional level in the Department of State and the three categories of the Foreign Service, only 204 were Negroes. Of these, 21 were counted among the 3,698 Foreign Service Officers proper, including 3 with the rank of ambassador. In the two decades following World War II, more than a dozen Negroes were assigned to ambassadorial posts, the first Negro accredited as an ambassador to other than an African state being sent to Norway in 1961.[11] In addition to those who have served in African countries, Negroes have also represented the United States as ambassadors in Finland, Luxemburg, and Syria, and in UN bodies.

One recurrent problem has been the feeling in some African quarters that since Negroes were regarded as second-class citizens in the United States, the sending of a Negro ambassador implied that Washington gave only second-class standing to the country to which he was assigned. Thus it is said that Ghana, coming to independence, let it be known that it did not want to receive a Negro ambassador, despite the praise of blackness and of the African Personality. This is no doubt a state of affairs which has already materially changed, but the heart of the matter is again that no satisfactory answer can be found short of the overcoming of racialism in the United States.

[10] Davis, *op. cit.*, p. 1, For much of the following material I have also drawn on Mr. Davis' paper with the same title, prepared for the second American Negro Leadership Conference on Africa, held in Washington, D.C., September 24-27, 1964.
[11] A number of Negro Americans had previously served as Ministers to Haiti.

6

Where Dangers Threaten

With thirty-nine independent states already established in Africa, and more slated to appear, it has been possible for the United States to work out significantly distinctive policies for each of them only gradually and tentatively. Indeed, since its relations with many of the states have been minimal, the United States has been able to operate largely on the basis of policies which were in principle Africa-wide or at least extended to a substantial number of states which fell in one or another grouping, although special circumstances have obviously called for special treatment. As each country carved out its separate identity, differentiating itself from the rest, it became increasingly necessary for the United States to respond by differentiating its policies accordingly. For the most part the way in which its relations with individual African states have been shaped has been of little general concern. Only in a few instances—notably in the Congo and the countries of southern Africa—has the United States become so deeply involved as to have a serious bearing on its general international position, affecting its relations with the UN and other states, African and non-African.

American policy toward Africa can certainly no longer be summed up in a general benevolent formula of self-determination, development, and good will, embracing the entire continent. For any meaningful analysis of the way in which African-American relations have developed it is necessary to look at the turn of events in particular states and the shaping of attitudes of particular circles of people within them. For this purpose it is possible, utilizing different criteria, to divide African states into groupings of different kinds whose members have tended to have a similar relationship with the United States. Any such allocation of states to groups must of course be undertaken in full awareness that it is an abstraction from a more complex and changing African reality in which the members shift their alignment from time to time, since African states are still far from having achieved fixity and stability of posture either internally or in their relations with each other. Of this there can be no more dramatic illustration than the coup of February, 1966, which overnight shifted Ghana from the radical to the more conservative column.

Four major lines of division among African states may be suggested, each cutting the pie somewhat differently, and with only two of them having a very significant bearing on relations with the United States. The first of those which has only minor bearing on African-American relations is the continuing great geographic divide which separates the states and peoples of West Africa from those in the East, where even the airplane has barely begun to break down the isolation of the two sides of the continent from each other. The second is the division between those countries which were under French colonial rule and those which were under the British. The ex-French and ex-British territories certainly make nothing approaching solid blocs since there are wide diversities of alignment within each of them, but bonds of language, culture, political structure, and shared memories exist, as well as more material ties, all of which have some effect in holding each of the two groupings together and maintaining ties with the former metropole. As far as the United States is concerned, access to the English-speaking countries has generally been easier than to those linked to France.

A further breakdown may be made to divide those states with a militant leftward, "progressive" slant from the larger, more moderate or conservative group which looks with less hostile eyes on the United States and the West in general. The best known of the militants were the states involved in the Guinea-Ghana-Mali union which was also linked to North African states in the Casablanca grouping. Congo-Brazzaville and perhaps Tanzania and one or two others should now be added to this fraternity. Even for the original three, however, the proposed union never came to fruition, and their solidarity was suspect even prior to Nkrumah's ouster, despite much similarity in ideological bent. Whatever the difficulty in pinning them down with precision and expecting them to stay pinned where they have been placed, a significant difference of real concern to the United States undoubtedly exists between those governments which look with complacency on friendly relations with the West and those which expect the insidious neo-colonialists to take them over if they are not constantly on guard. An added complication in thus attempting to mark off the militants from the more relaxed is that in each country a number of people hold views sharply opposed to those of the ruling circles. The most evident or, at all events, the most audible disparities of outlook between government and some elements of the citizenry are to be found in the conservatively-inclined countries, such as several of the ex-French territories, where a substantial body of dissidents calls for more radical, socialistic, Africanizing, and pan-African policies. In Nigeria this type of demand contributed to the military coup of January, 1966.

Potentially by far the most important division separates white-dominated southern Africa from the independent African states north of Angola and Mozambique. A neater geographic line which gave the vast white-dominated area an even greater expanse and compactness has already been breached through the disintegration of the Rhodesia-Nyasaland Federation in 1963, which cleared the way for the independence of Zambia and Malawi, thrusting a black African wedge southward. The Republic of South Africa and its disputed adjoining mandated territory of Southwest Africa, however, still have bulwarks between themselves and independent Black Africa to the north, and will have them so long as Rhodesia and the Portuguese territories deny rule to their African majorities. Britain's grant of independence in 1966 to the enclaves of Bechuanaland and Basutoland under their new names of Botswana and Lesotho, to be followed shortly by independence for Swaziland, brings African-run states into the closest contact with South Africa, but the present presumption is that the dependence of these states on South Africa is so great as virtually to ensure their good behavior. If this proves in fact to be the case, South Africa would have no occasion to stir up further international trouble by any overt action against them. On the other hand, attacks on apartheid stemming from these countries could lead to swift reprisals, and the imposition of sanctions on South Africa might lead to their being swallowed up.

These are the two great adversaries, white-dominated Africa to the south and independent black Africa to the north. At some not-too-distant time the United States may find itself confronted by the stark alternative of embracing one Africa or the other as the two move into more overt and bitter conflict with each other.

For the future the most explosive threat to the peace of Africa is without question South Africa's detested policy of apartheid, bolstered as it is by neighboring Rhodesia and the Portuguese colonies. For the last few years, however, it is the Congo which has most threatened the continent's peace, although Rhodesia's declaration of independence on November 11, 1965 opened up a new battleground, potentially involving South Africa as well. When the Congo began to fall apart at all its seams on the morrow of independence, the Cold War overtly intruded itself into the continent for the first time, and the threat of white military intervention became a reality. Since the African states were divided among themselves, and often each within itself, on Congolese issues, the United States found itself embroiled in bitterest African controversy when, openly and behind the scenes, it stepped into the thick of the Congo's troubles.

THE CONGO

It is the Congo, more than any other single part of Africa, which has been the scene of America's most serious fall from grace in the eyes of many Africans. It is, of course, no matter of coincidence that the Congo was also the one African country in which the United States has most actively intervened.[1]

The importance of the Congo derives from the fact that it is a vast and richly endowed territory, bordering on nine other African countries and reaching deep into the heart of Africa. It is inhabited by some 14 million people of many tribes and languages who suddenly achieved independence on June 30, 1960 but had virtually no experience which could fit them for the running of a modern state or endow them with a sense of national identity. Taken over in 1908 by the Belgian government from the exploitation and maladministration of King Leopold, which had become an international scandal, the Congo's mineral and other riches came to be relatively highly developed, while its people were placed under the wing of a paternalistic colonial administration, tightly controlled from Brussels. Assuming that the colonial authorities had lived up to their best intentions, it is arguable that in another half century an admirably prepared Congolese population might have been ready to join in more or less equal partnership with the metropole. Instead of half a century, Belgium and the Congo had a year and a half to get ready for independence after rioting broke out in Leopoldville in January, 1959. The result was the independence of a population with, in African terms, a fairly high level of at least nominal literacy but in 1959-1960 only 28,900 children were enrolled in secondary schools, of which more than half were Belgians, and no more than a tiny handful of Congolese had received higher education. No Congolese figured in the upper brackets of the colonial administration; and the armed forces, so shortly to be the center of attention, had no Congolese officers. The first elections in the Congo were held in cautious fashion at the communal level in 1957, and no political parties had been allowed.

What moved the Belgian government to make so hasty a retreat when it was challenged by the Leopoldville riots and by difficulties elsewhere? No doubt part was panic, and part was calculation. The element of panic came from the fact that the troubles were largely unexpected, plus the recognition that in some areas the situation was getting so far out of hand that the government no longer had effective control. Certainly the Belgians, warned by the example of Algeria, had no stomach for a long and and bitter colonial war. The element of calculation—the so-called *pari congolais* or bet on the Congo—derived from what appeared to be the very strong position held by the Belgians who controlled the government, the army, and the economy, and had trained almost no Congolese to replace them. It was possible to conclude that for any foreseeable future, independence would be a largely formal matter with some Congolese enjoying the pomp and ceremony of the top offices while the Belgians went on running the show. What many Belgians expected to be the situation in the Congo at large was probably well illustrated in Katanga after Moise

[1] I am indebted to Dean Edmund A Gullion of the Fletcher School of Law and Diplomacy, U.S. Ambassador to the Congo under President Kennedy, for a number of valuable suggestions concerning this section on the Congo, for which, of course, he has no other responsibility.

Tshombe's declaration of independence on July 11, 1960. Although official Belgian recognition of Katanga as a state was never given, Belgian economic support and civilian and military personnel were available, and the Union Minière was doing very nicely. In the rest of the Congo the mutinies and succeeding disorders drove out not only the Belgian officers, but also the bulk of the Belgian civilian population, who fled in panic.

American political and economic involvement in the Congo prior to independence was slight. Belgium had an overwhelmingly large share of the private investment of some $2.5 billion, while American direct investment came to less than 1 per cent of the total. After June 30, 1960, the United States was immediately drawn in and has become more rather than less deeply involved as the years have gone by, finding itself in an extraordinary turn of events in 1964-1965, giving extensive backing to the same Tshombe, as Congolese Premier, whom it had earlier deemed necessary to oust as the leading figure in secessionist Katanga. The American role in the Congo since independence has been of central importance, whether the United States worked through the UN, as it generally did up to the departure of the UN force in mid-1964, or operated largely unilaterally as in the succeeding phase.

The disintegration which threatened the Congo on the heels of independence led both to armed intervention by Belgian paratroopers and to a frenzied search by the newly installed Congolese government for support. Appeals to the United States met with the response that the UN was the appropriate instrumentality for action, and that the Powers should be kept from direct intervention. On July 14, 1960, the first Security Council resolution on the Congo was adopted with the backing of the Soviet Union and the United States but with abstentions by France and Great Britain. Calling for the withdrawal of Belgian troops and authorizing the Secretary-General to provide the Congo with military assistance, the resolution brought into existence, within an amazing thirty-six hours —thanks in part to an American airlift operating from European bases—a UN force in which the Great Powers did not participate.

What lay behind the determination of the United States to work through the UN rather than to act unilaterally was given sophisticated expression a year later by Adlai E. Stevenson, United States Representative to the UN, who contended that any direct intervention by the West would have been interpreted as an attempt to reimpose colonial rule. In his opinion, the Cold War could be kept out of the Congo only by keeping the UN in, but beyond this, he saw the UN as "the only instrument by which the end of the Western system of colonialism can be prevented from opening the doors to the new imperialism of the East." [2]

The American decision to abstain from direct intervention, although the CIA was reputed to have engaged in various ventures, and to turn to the UN for the handling of the problems of the Congo was one of major importance for all parties concerned. Among other things, it signaled the readiness of the United States to settle for a neutralist Congo rather than

[2] Stevenson, "The United Nations, First Step Towards a World Under Law," *Department of State Bulletin*, XLV, No. 1149 (July 10, 1961), 68-71.

to seek its enlistment in the American camp in the earlier spirit of John Foster Dulles. In the case of Korea, it might not unjustly be said that the United States *used* the UN as an instrument of its policies, furnishing the bulk of the armed forces and the military and political leadership, whereas in the Congo neither American forces nor an American military command was involved. Although the decision to turn to the UN obviously involved a gamble, the United States was presumably confident that on matters of ultimate importance it could generally count on having its own way, as in fact it usually did.[3] No doubt the Russians also had hopes that they would be able to control the UN's operations in the Congo through their fraternal association with the anti-colonial Afro-Asian bloc. Their failure led to Moscow's embittered and unsuccessful insistence on having a veto over all active operating roles of the UN by substituting a "troika" for the Secretary-General and by renewing the emphasis on the Security Council.

The two great functions of the UN in the Congo were to serve as a neutralizing presence standing between the Powers and to save the Congo from total disintegration. On the first score, the threatened confrontation of the Soviet Union and the United States in the Congo was averted, and a number of other clashes of policy, including some among African states, were kept within a manageable framework. On the second score, the survival of the Congo, even in its present battered state, is due in very large measure to the massive UN assistance program to which the United States made heavy contributions. Beyond any reasonable argument, what the situation really called for was the imposition of a firm trusteeship which would hold the country together while its leadership was being trained and its new institutions shaped, but this was both politically and legally excluded. A grievous failure, however, was the unreadiness or inability of the UN to secure the disarming of the Force Publique and the building of an effective military force on which the Congolese government could rely. If the sheer magnitude of the task the UN took on strained the organization close to the breaking point, it is difficult to imagine the fate of the Congo if the UN had not become so deeply involved in its affairs.

The range of UN action was limited by Hammarskjold's contention that while the organization was committed to the maintenance of law and order, it was also bound by the Security Council resolution of August 9, 1960, which laid it down that "the United Nations force in the Congo will not be a party to or in any way intervene in or be used to influence the outcome of any internal conflict, constitutional or otherwise." In his view the UN could resort to the use of force only in self-defense and was

[3] Conor Cruse O'Brien, a participant in the UN's Congo activities, contended that while the United States had lost the almost automatic control over the UN which it had had up to 1957, it still, at the time he wrote in 1963, could exercise "a sophisticated kind of parliamentary diplomacy" to win Afro-Asian support for its policies by negotiation. (*Conflicting Concepts of the United Nations*. Leeds: Leeds University, 1964, pp. 4-6. See also his *To Katanga and Back: A UN Case History*. London: Hutchinson, 1962.) On the other hand, the American Congo policy was irresponsibly attacked at home by some opponents as enabling the USSR to utilize the UN as a Trojan horse for entry into the Congo.

bound to observe strict neutrality in relation to Congolese parties and factions.

Nowhere did the handicaps which this interpretation imposed show themselves more flagrantly than in the two vitally important problems of the treatment of Patrice Lumumba and of secessionist Katanga, in both of which the United States had a large stake.[4]

Throughout Africa, and far more widely in the world at large, Lumumba, the Congo's first Prime Minister, was hailed as the outstanding champion of Congolese national unity and independence and as a martyr in the anti-colonial struggle. Since the United States had come to take an increasingly hostile attitude toward him, primarily because of his call for Communist support, it was accused, as the ally of Belgium and the leader of the imperialists, of having a major share in the ultimate responsibility for his murder in Katanga early in 1961. Pro-Lumumbist demonstrations were held in many places in Africa and elsewhere, directed at least in part against the United States and its alleged complicity in his death. America's standing plummeted to a new low in many African quarters, and particularly in those with a leftward inclination.

The ultimate turn of events in Katanga helped to restore the good name of the United States, but the earlier failure of the UN to take any decisive action against Tshombe's separatist grip on this richest of Congo provinces led to a linking of Katanga with the murder of Lumumba as a demonstration of the insatiable imperialist search for profits and domination. As early as its resolution of August 9, 1960, the Security Council called for the speedy withdrawal of Belgian troops from Katanga and declared that the entry of the UN Force into the province was necessary, but Katanga was not effectively brought within the Congolese fold until early 1963.

The American position on Katanga hardened with the take-over by the Kennedy administration, which was more inclined than its predecessor to lend a sympathetic ear to the fears and desires of other African countries in relation to the Congo. In the last days of 1962 the breaking point was reached after a long series of false starts and futile negotiations, including the American-sponsored meeting between Tshombe and Premier Adoula at Kitona in December, 1961, and U Thant's plan of August, 1962, for a federal solution. With full American backing and despite continued British and French opposition, the UNF in January, 1963, re-established the unity of the Congo, ridding Katanga of its mercenaries while Tshombe went into exile. The Assistant Secretary of State for African Affairs, G. Mennen Williams, emphasized the importance of the event, holding that "It did more to restore African confidence in the United Nations and the West—and particularly in the United States—than any other event in

[4] The intricacies of the situation have been explored by several writers. See, for example, Stanley Hoffmann, "In Search of a Thread: The UN in the Congo Labyrinth," *International Organization*, XVI, No. 2 (1962), 331-61; Catherine Hoskyns, *The Congo: A Chronology of Events, January 1960-December 1961* (London: Royal Institute of International Affairs, 1962); King Gordon, *The U.N. in the Congo* (New York: Carnegie Endowment for International Peace, 1962); Ernest W. Lefever, *Crisis in the Congo: A U.N. Force in Action* (Washington, D.C.: Brookings, 1965).

the last five years." [5] Within the United States, however, the government's policy in relation to Katanga had come in for bitter criticism both from peace groups which questioned the use of force by the UN and by backers of NATO who felt that the United States was endangering its major alliance. While Washington and its supporters warned of the danger that the Communists would make the cause of Congolese unity their own if the UN did not take vigorous action with full American backing, its opponents, including a well-financed Katanga lobby, protested that Katanga was the one safe anti-Communist bulwark in the Congo. A point of key importance was that Katanga's revenues, withheld by Tshombe, constituted a very large share of the total income of the Congo and were necessary for its survival. For the successful functioning of the Congo as a whole, as well as to eliminate an endless source of trouble and agitation, it was essential that Katanga be rejoined to the state of which it formed a part.

Having attained this goal, the UN promptly began to reduce its committment in the Congo although the United States urged, successfully for a time, that there should be no precipitate withdrawal of the UNF. The Congo's times of trouble were far from being over, but the failure to find an internationally acceptable means of financing the operation and, more formally, the ultimate lack of an invitation from the Congo government for the UNF to remain led to the withdrawal of the last UN troops in June, 1964. The end of the military operations in the Congo did not, however, mean the end of what had become the largest assistance operation ever attempted by international organizations.

As the date set for the departure of the UNF came nearer, the United States began to extend its unilateral operations in the Congo in order to deal with situations which grew increasingly difficult and threatening. The two central features in the new turn of events were the spread of rebel activity and Tshombe's spectacular return from exile in June, 1964, to be named Prime Minister by President Kasavubu early in July.

Even before the UNF withdrawal, the United States was involved in the Congo's efforts to curb rebel advances, not only through the provision of military material and a small training program, but also through the temporary employment of a few American civilian pilots to fly combat missions against the rebels, reputed to be receiving Chinese aid and direction.[6]

The return of Tshombe and his elevation to head the government were

[5] See his succinct review of "Congo Realities and United States Policy," Department of State Press Release, No. 84 (April 23, 1965), p. 8. Mr. Williams added that the successful United States-supported UN action thwarted a Soviet move to end Katangan secession by violent means, thus denying the USSR "a sure, popular, and Africa-wide approved return to power and influence in the Congo."

[6] An explicit denial by the State Department that Americans supposedly on training missions in the Congo were flying in combat was followed by an embarrassed admission that it had in fact been taking place. The next day it was announced that American citizens would fly no more combat missions in the Congo. The use of Americans for such purposes, as well as of Cuban exiles flying combat and transport planes, was presumably an enterprise of the Central Intelligence Agency. See *The New York Times*, June 17, 18, 1964; April 27, 1966.

a source of embarrassment to Washington. Despite charges that the United States was engaged in an imperialist plot with Belgium and others to bring Tshombe back, it was well known, as Assistant Secretary of State Williams mildly put it, that "his relations with a number of African leaders, as well as with us, were less than cordial." [7] The United States, now with Johnson as President and a change of ambassadors in Leopoldville, was, however, prepared to accept Tshombe in his new post as a man of ability who could be counted on to combat the Communists. This acceptance was undertaken in full knowledge of Tshombe's intrigues with the Communist powers and the collaboration of his supporters with the Communist-backed parties in the effort to oust the Adoula government. It was also well known that many Africans regarded Tshombe as having stained his hands in the blood of Lumumba, and as being an agent of the big Belgian financial interests and notably of the Union Minière.

In August, 1964, in the face of rebel advances which the still demoralized Congolese national army (ANC) was unable to resist, including the fall of Stanleyville and the seizure of many hostages, American officials saw the Congo coming apart at the seams and agreed to step up military and other aid. Tshombe's appeal to several of the more conservative African states for military aid was rejected, and African hostility to him was intensified by his resort again, as earlier in Katanga, to the recruitment as mercenaries of white South Africans, Rhodesians, and embittered Algerian Frenchmen. The officially stated American position was that while the United States neither condoned nor approved of hiring white mercenaries, it acknowledged the legal right of the Congo to do so and hoped that their services could soon be dispensed with. [8]

American military aid was increased in the form not only of transport planes and helicopters, but also of a small number of paratroopers whose mission was announced as one of guarding the planes and not engaging in combat; but anti-Castro Cuban pilots were flying combat missions in American-supplied planes. Inevitably questions were raised as to whether the United States was not embarking on a venture which might escalate to turn the Congo into an African Vietnam, but the American authorities stood firm against being drawn seriously into the fighting despite the charges of Communist involvement on the rebel side.

The climax of this phase of the Congo's affairs—and of African bitterness against the United States—was reached with the Stanleyville paratroop drop of November 24, 1964. The fact that this operation was undertaken just as Tshombe's forces, spearheaded by the mercenaries, were moving on Stanleyville is explained on the American side as deriving from the fear that the arrival of the ANC would be the signal for a massacre of the hostages and condemned by the opponents of the operation as a concerted military move to ensure that the city would fall to Tshombe. Ambassador Stevenson later informed the Security Council that 2,000 people of many nationalities, including Asians and Africans, were rescued, but some hostages were killed in the interval between the paratroop drop

[7] Williams, "Congo Realities," p. 10.
[8] G. Mennen Williams, "U.S. Objectives in the Congo, 1960-65," *Africa Report*, X, No. 8 (August, 1965), 19.

and the actual rescue. It is an insoluble "if," to which sharply divergent answers have been given, whether the rescue operation in fact saved more lives than might have been saved without it.

In American, and more generally in Western, eyes, this was a humanitarian venture, made unavoidable by the brutal tactics of the rebels and the failure of negotiations to free the hostages. Official spokesmen emphasized that it was backed by an invitation from Tshombe and was carried out expeditiously with a minimum of loss and damage. In much of Africa and elsewhere it was seen as imperialist intervention to aid Tshombe and his white mercenaries break the back of a popular rising in the Congo at a time when negotiations were still in progress. To make matters worse, the troops employed were again the Belgian paratroopers whose reappearance in the Congo just after independence had roused such hostility and who had also been called in by Tshombe to bolster his declaration of Katanga's independence.

The versions that were given by opposing spokesmen seemed scarcely to relate to the same episode. Thus Adlai Stevenson spoke of:

> The grim story of thousands of innocent civilians—many of them foreign —illegally seized, brutalized, and threatened, and many murdered by rebels against the Congo government. . . . Every means—legal, moral, and humane, including the United Nations—was exhausted to protect their lives and secure their release—all without avail. When it became apparent that there was no hope, the Belgian and American governments, with the cooperation of the Government of the United Kingdom, and with the express authorization of the sovereign government of the Democratic Republic of the Congo, undertook an emergency rescue mission to save the lives of these innocent people. The operation was carried out with restraint, courage, discipline, and dispatch.[9]

Among the attackers of the operation was the Congo (Brazzaville) Foreign Minister, Charles Ganao, who asked:

> What humanitarian principles are at stake, when, on the pretext of saving the lives of an insignificant number of whites, tens of thousands of blacks are massacred—innocent blacks who know nothing of political manoeuvres and whose only crime is that of having been born in a country whose natural resources are shockingly plentiful? . . . The Stanleyville aggression is an extremely serious matter. It has proved, in striking fashion, that there is no place for the black man in this world wherever he may be, whether it be in a country to which he came in the same way as others before him, or in his own homeland of Africa. Indeed, it is sufficient for a minority of white imperialists and racists to appear anywhere, for the black man to find himself deprived of every right, even the right to live. Now, even in his own country, even in a country with a black Government, the black man no longer feels safe.[10]

[9] Statement before the Security Council (*The New York Times*, December 14, 1964).

[10] *Security Council Official Records*, 1170 (December 9, 1964), pp. 14-16. *Time* repaid African vituperation in kind on December 4, 1964, with the assertion that the death of the American missionary, Dr. Carlson, and others at the hands of "a rabble

The Ghanaian Foreign Minister asked what the American reaction would be if Ghana sent a military force to the southern states to help Negroes who were being tortured because they demanded their rights.

Throughout December the Security Council, in a series of sessions marked by unparalleled vituperation and charges and countercharges of racism, debated an accusation brought by eighteen African states and four others that the Belgian-American action was a flagrant violation of the Charter and a threat to the peace and security of Africa. Although the debate revealed a stored-up hostility to the United States, which came as a shock to American opinion, the end result was more favorable than had seemed likely. With no specific mention of the paratroop drop the resolution which was adopted on December 30, 1964, with only France abstaining, asked for an end to intervention in the Congo's domestic affairs, a cease-fire, and the withdrawal of the mercenaries, and entrusted the Organization of African Unity with the task of achieving national integration in the Congo.

The United States continued to provide military and other assistance to Tshombe's Congo, and, with American approval, substantial numbers of Belgians returned in a variety of advisory and other guises. For many Africans and some African governments, Tshombe remained a pariah, and American support for him rendered the United States even more suspect than before as the outstanding neo-colonialist power; but Nigeria and a number of other countries, including particularly many of those formerly under French rule, were prepared to accept Tshombe's claim to legitimacy, laying stress on the injunction in the OAU Charter against intervention in the domestic affairs of African states. In this stand they had the backing of de Gaulle as well as of Portugal and South Africa.

The Stanleyville episode made the American position more difficult and more subject to attack than before but prejudiced it less universally and lastingly than seemed likely at first blush. Tshombe's success in securing, at least superficially, a measure of pacification and stability in the Congo no doubt helped to overcome some African hostility both to him and to American support for him; but his term of office was to be relatively brief. In October, 1965 President Kasavubu dismissed him from the Prime Ministership, only himself to be dismissed as President when General Mobutu took over the government in a coup on November 25, 1965.

The tangled and unhappy affairs of the Congo have shed little glory on anyone. For the United States it has been an expensive operation in a number of ways. In material terms alone the United States had given more than $400 million in various forms of aid to the Congo by the time of the withdrawal of the UN Force in mid-1964, but the other costs are perhaps even more substantial. Yet, in the results, to date, the country's unity has been preserved, it has made at least the beginnings of recovery

---

of dazed, ignorant savages," proved that "Black African civilization—with its elaborate trappings of half a hundred sovereignties, governments, and U.N. delegations is largely a pretense" and wondered "whether Black Africa can be taken seriously at all, or whether, for the foreseeable future, it is beyond the reach of reason."

or advance on several social and economic fronts with massive foreign assistance primarily from Belgium, the United States, and the UN, and the American goal of preventing a Communist take-over has so far been achieved.

PORTUGUESE AFRICAN COLONIES

The problems presented by the Portuguese territories in Africa differed radically in almost every significant respect from those of the Congo. Although both areas created difficulties for the United States, the Portuguese situation invited no direct and overt American intervention of the kind which took place in the Congo. In both instances it is evident that much has gone on behind the scenes; but as far as the public record goes, the greater part of the American entanglement with Portuguese Africa has consisted of speeches and votes in the UN. If the direct economic and political concern of the United States with the Portuguese territories was slight, it was a matter of central consequence that Portugal was a NATO ally, that it was supplied with American arms, and that the American military stressed the importance of the base in the Azores established through somewhat precarious agreement with Portugal.

In contrast to the single vast territory of the Congo, the Portuguese holdings consisted of five separate entities: the Cape Verde Islands, São Tome and Principe, Portuguese Guinea, Angola, and Mozambique. Of these, only Angola and Mozambique—with populations, respectively, of upwards of five and seven million—constitute large African domains, although Portuguese Guinea has also been a source of political friction. The importance of Angola and Mozambique derived not only from the size of their land mass and population, but also from their positions as the northernmost bastions of white-controlled southern Africa and from Angola's long common frontier with the Congo.

Portuguese colonial policy differed significantly from that of the other colonial powers in Africa, save perhaps Spain. A dictatorship at home, under the long-lived Salazar, Portugal virtually closed the doors to political participation on the part of its African masses and was disinclined to tolerate any political movements. If Portuguese policy here resembled Belgium's in its centralization and paternalism, it diverged sharply from the Belgian treatment of the Congo in its relative lack of economic development and the meagerness of the educational and social advantages which it offered. On the educational score, for example, it has been estimated that at the start of the 1960's only 1 per cent or 2 per cent of the African population of Angola and Mozambique had achieved literacy. Indeed, Africans have been heard to ask what was to be expected when the metropole itself had a high rate of illiteracy, still lingered at a relatively low level of economic development, and was possessed of no political freedom.

On the other hand, Portugal repudiated the South African pattern of racial discrimination and segregation, proclaiming that it set up no color bars but welcomed on equal terms all who achieved appropriate standards of Western-style civilization, the so-called *assimilados*. The catch was that only a few thousands among the millions of Africans were accepted as civilized, and the educational and other facilities which would multiply their numbers were scanty. The situation was made even more difficult by the fact that it was—and is—Lisbon's policy to strengthen the Portuguese presence in Africa, particularly in Angola, by sending out Portuguese settlers, including peasants and workers, who took over land and jobs to which Africans might lay claim, inevitably producing racial grievances. The situation was aggravated by the repeated charge, occasionally taking on the dimensions of an international scandal, that Portugal tolerated or promoted a system of forced labor in its colonies.

Portugal's policy and practice made it singularly difficult for her to deal with the issues raised by the era of anti-colonialism on terms acceptable to the new molders of world opinion. No doubt because it saw that era moving in, Portugal in 1951 by a stroke of the pen had removed the label of colonialism from its relations with its overseas territories and declared them all to be provinces of a single unified Portuguese state and nation. Thereafter, despite the fact that the substance of the colonial bonds had not been changed and the great bulk of the Africans remained "natives" and not citizens, Lisbon defended resolutely the thesis that Portugal possessed no colonies and that therefore no issue of self-determination was involved.

Upon Portugal's admission to the UN in December, 1955, this stand led her into mounting conflict with the new-style majority and forced the United States to take decisions which it would no doubt have been delighted to evade. The question promptly arose whether Portugal was responsible for the administration of non-self-governing territories. If so, it was obligated under the Charter to develop self-government and free political institutions in such territories, and to report on their economic, social, and educational conditions. In sum, what was called for was the acceptance by Portugal of a measure of international accountability for carrying out in its imperial domains a kind of policy to which it was fundamentally opposed. In denying any UN jurisdiction, Portugal was to find its best defense, not in the substance of its position, but in the important procedural issue concerning the right of the General Assembly to substitute its judgment as to the constitutional status of a territory for that of the state directly concerned.[11]

For four or five years after taking up its UN membership, Portugal and its Western supporters, including the United States, were able to hold off the attack; but by an Assembly resolution adopted in December, 1960, the United States abstaining, every overseas Portuguese territory was named as non-self-governing and hence subject to the reporting provisions of Chapter XI. Portugal remained recalcitrant, and the increasingly independence-minded UN majority had in fact no means of enforcing its verdict. From that time forward, however, the pressure mounted as a series of steps were taken by UN bodies to investigate conditions in

[11] For a statement of the arguments pro and con in relation to the applicability of Chapter XI, see Patricia Wohlgemuth, *The Portuguese Territories and the United Nations* (New York: Carnegie Endowment for International Peace, International Conciliation No. 545, November, 1963).

Portuguese Africa, to propose reforms with growing urgency, and to demand that Portugal grant the right of self-determination.

In 1961 a drastic change in the situation shifted attention from UN debates to the African colonies themselves. On February 4 some hundreds of Africans attacked the police barracks in Luanda, capital of Angola, leaving behind them a substantial number of dead and wounded when the rioting subsided, and in the following month a larger scale and still smoldering rebellion broke out in northeastern Angola. In contrast to the Belgian decision to move speedily to independence for the Congo after the Leopoldville riots two years earlier, Portugal adopted a policy of all-out repression. Portuguese troops were sent to Angola at a cost which Lisbon could ill afford, and the whites in the colony were armed as vigilantes, while the security forces were strengthened in Mozambique, which was increasingly threatened as rebel forces were organized.

From Portugal's standpoint these risings came at a peculiarly bad time, and the Portuguese plea that all the troubles were inspired by alien agitators carried little conviction. The number of anti-colonial states in the UN had grown amazingly; and Britain, France, and Belgium, largely or wholly divested of their colonial responsibilities, no longer felt the same pressure to defend colonial positions. Furthermore, Angola's bloody upheavals coincided with the change from the Eisenhower to the Kennedy administration in Washington, bringing in a greater sympathy with Africa and a disinclination to stand up and be counted in support of Portugal. As the years went by, however, it became apparent that the role which Washington found most congenial was trying to mediate between the Afro-Asians and the Portuguese in a usually vain effort to keep everybody happy and to keep the United States less than fully committed to either side.

The move toward UN action followed close on the heels of the Angolan outbreaks. One of the first and bitterest blows to Portugal came when the United States in March, 1961, voted in the Security Council with the USSR and the United Arab Republic as well as Liberia and Ceylon for a resolution, defeated by the abstention of the other six members, which called for reforms in Angola and asked for a UN inquiry there, citing the recent risings. The United States was attacked both for the stand it took in voting and for its failure to consult Portugal and others of its allies; but *The New York Times* on March 18 editorially praised what it saw as "in a very real sense, a new declaration of American independence" which, without weakening loyalty to NATO, enabled the United States to criticize the colonial policies of even its closest friends when it held them to be wrong. A few days later the United States joined in backing the submission of the Angolan question to General Assembly debate, and voted for an Assembly resolution adopted on April 20, 1961, which found the situation in Angola likely to endanger the maintenance of international peace and security, asked Portugal to live up to the 1960 UN declaration on colonial independence, and authorized a subcommittee to inquire into Angolan affairs. On June 9 the United States somewhat unhappily cast its vote with a majority of nine in the Security Council, Britain and France abstaining, for a resolution which condemned Portugal's repressive measures in Angola, reaffirmed the April Assembly resolution, and called upon Portugal to "desist forthwith from repressive measures."

The dilemma which confronted the United States can be illustrated by two diametrically opposed lines of attack on American policy. Premier Salazar on June 30, 1961, accused the General Assembly of operating by mob rule, said that he had no intention of complying with the resolution calling on Portugal to stop fighting and to collaborate with the committee of inquiry, and denounced the United States as both weakening Europe's defenses and violating its NATO obligations.[12] Just a month earlier, on May 30, President Nkrumah had laid before the Ghanaian Parliament his version of the international financial interests which dominated the Angolan scene and found what he termed the Portuguese colonial dictatorship immensely strengthened by its NATO membership. "Portugal," he continued, "is only able to wage a colonial war because fundamentally she has the backing of the North Atlantic Treaty Organization. If this backing were withdrawn tomorrow and Portugal was excluded from NATO, Portugal's colonial rule would collapse the day after."[13]

Although the record thereafter is spotty, 1961 appears to have marked the high point of American collaboration with the Afro-Asian forces in the UN in relation to the Portuguese territories. Owing both to the crossfire to which it found itself subjected at home and abroad and to the increasingly belligerent attitude of the anti-colonial majority, the United States characteristically swung to a middle-of-the-road position in which it sought to moderate the language of resolutions and bring about some sort of negotiated solution. American statements and actions left no doubt of Washington's disapproval of Portugal's colonial policy, but also made quite clear that the United States was not easily to be drawn into denunciations and sanctions. The American view was laid out in July, 1964, by J. Wayne Fredericks, Deputy Assistant Secretary of State for African Affairs:

> We in the United States are deeply committed to self-determination for all people. We believe Portugal should recognize publicly that the principle of self-determination is applicable to its territories. Our policy is to encourage both Portugal and the Africans to come to a workable understanding.[14]

African and Portuguese interpretations of what was involved in self-determination were so flatly opposed to each other as to render American efforts at mediation and moderation essentially fruitless. Under the pressure of world opinion and of the continued warfare in Angola, Portugal has indeed introduced a number of reforms, but they were still far

[12] *The New York Times,* July 1, 1961.
[13] *The Party* (Accra), June, 1961.
[14] Cited by Waldemar A. Nielsen, *African Battleline: American Policy Choices in Southern Africa* (New York: Harper, 1965), p. 29.

removed from the independence on which the Africans insisted. In a move potentially of great significance, full citizenship was bestowed on all natives of the overseas provinces instead of being reserved for the assimilated few. Educational opportunities at all levels have been increased, changes in labor policy have dealt with some of the major abuses, and economic development has been speeded. In the political sphere there has been a multiplication and strengthening of councils and of representation at various levels, but no real extension of democratic participation in the conduct of affairs. Within the framework of the unity of the total Portuguese domain, steps have been taken which look toward the establishment of some measure of provincial autonomy. When all the reforms have been added together, however, it remains to be seen whether they represent a fundamental change in the highly unsatisfactory pre-1961 situation, and certainly they fall far short of minimum demands on the part of the anti-colonialists.

The way in which events have moved in the UN can be illustrated by glancing at the provisions of resolution S/5380 adopted by the Security Council on July 31, 1963. Recalling a series of earlier Assembly and Council resolutions, the resolution reaffirmed that the Portuguese territories were non-self-governing, and it deprecated Portugal's repeated violations of the principles of the Charter. It called upon Portugal to recognize the right of its territories to self-determination and independence, to cease all acts of repression and withdraw all forces employed for that purpose, and to take several specified steps, such as an unconditional political amnesty, with a view to the transfer of power to freely elected political institutions and the grant of independence immediately thereafter. All states were requested by the resolution to:

> refrain forthwith from offering the Portuguese Government any assistance which would enable it to continue its repression of the peoples of the territories under its administration, and to take all measures to prevent the sale and supply of arms and military equipment for this purpose to the Portuguese Government.[15]

A number of key words and phrases of this resolution were the product of prolonged debate and negotiation in an effort to work out terms which would secure a maximum of agreement among the council's members. A major compromise was the abandonment of a mandatory embargo on arms and other aid for Portugal in favor of a recommendation without binding force. Even with the modifications which they were able to secure in the original statement, the United States, Britain, and France, Portugal's major allies, abstained in the final vote. Thus the powers most likely to furnish large-scale military assistance were not only free of any legal obligation to comply, but also had indicated their lack of approval of the measure. Furthermore, the terms of the resolution made it possible to furnish any form of aid to Portugal if it were not used for

[15] As early as General Assembly Resolution 1742 (XVI) of January 30, 1962, all members of the UN and the specialized agencies had been requested "to deny to Portugal any support and assistance which may be used by it for the suppression of the people of Angola."

the purpose of continuing suppression; and it was the American contention that arms supplied under NATO auspices could not be utilized in Angola or other overseas territories.

American policy in relation to Portugal was the resultant of pushes and pulls in every direction. Left and liberal opinion favored stronger moves, while conservatives with more of an eye to Europe and the Cold War sought to protect Portugal from the anti-colonialist bloc. With less success, and presumably with less financial backing than the propagandists for Tshombe's Katanga, the Portuguese employed an American public relations firm to work on American opinion.[16] Little propaganda was needed for those who saw the menace of Communism as the predominant issue, since they took it to be a self-evident absurdity for the United States to side against an anti-Communist Christian country which was holding the fort in Africa, particularly when the American partners in UN voting included the Soviet Union, Indonesia, Ghana, and the United Arab Republic. A special source of pressure on the United States derived from the fact that the agreement with Portugal for American use of military facilities in the Azores ran out at the end of 1962, and Portugal declined to renew it, preferring to let the United States stay on on an *ad hoc* basis, subject to pressure at any time. Portugal bitterly resented what it saw as American desertion, and American military authorities regarded the Azores as vitally important, although it was also true that Portugal received substantial benefits from the existence of the base and that—particularly under changing military and logistical conditions—other authorities were more skeptical as to the American need for the Azores.

One of the gravest difficulties was that while it was clear that Portugal had not prepared the people under its rule to govern themselves, there was little reason to think that if Portuguese rule were extended it would now effectively carry through the job which it had barely started in its centuries of colonial dominance. Both the ability and the willingness to speed social, economic, and political development were in question. The Portuguese were certainly not unaware that the advancement of colonial peoples had everywhere served ultimately not to bring assimilation and political acquiescence but rather to stimulate the nationalist demand for independence.

Nor, if Portugal were eliminated, was there any other authority which might be relied on for tutelage or guidance. The UN seemed most unlikely to repeat the experience it had gone through in the Congo, although it and its affiliated agencies were aiding the large numbers of refugees who had fled from Portuguese territories to independent neighboring countries and carrying on a modest program of training Africans for the roles which independence would require. The African states were often insistent that the problem was essentially an African one, but it was highly dubious that they were organized or united enough to take on the task of guidance and development of vast territories, perhaps complicated by a need for extensive policing.

[16] For an account of testimony given the Senate Foreign Relations Committee as to Portuguese publicity efforts, see *The New York Times*, July 24, 1963.

To the surprise of many, and maybe even of the Portuguese themselves, the pressure was eased by two factors: (1) the faltering of the rebel movement in Angola, which had never significantly spread beyond the Bakongo of the northeast and (2) the slow start of the attack upon Portuguese rule in Mozambique. The Portuguese suppression of the Angolan rebellion has been both ruthless and effective, and the opposing forces have not been able to achieve unity in opposition, nor has aid from the OAU been adequate to halt the loss of morale and momentum. For Angola, one factor which entered in was the American-aided taking over of the Congo by Tshombe who showed little enthusiasm for rebel movements based in his country. It is difficult to imagine that at some point the forces of African nationalism will not be victorious, but in the first rounds the Portuguese appeared to have the situation largely under control.

RHODESIA

When Prime Minister Ian Smith of Southern Rhodesia on November 11, 1965 finally issued his unilateral declaration of independence (UDI), he challenged the world to swing into action against the government of one of the key countries composing the white-dominated complex of southern Africa. The issues directly raised by Rhodesia's defiance of Britain were significant enough in themselves, but it was impossible not to see it also as a portent of far graver things to come: a curtain-raiser for South Africa's ultimate conflict with most of the rest of the world over apartheid and as a small-scale trial run of how that conflict might be carried on and what it might involve.

The response to UDI was immediate, although whether it was adequate was a matter of much greater dispute. Great Britain denounced the action as illegal, invalid, and treasonable, and was joined by the United States both in denunciation of this "spurious declaration of independence" by a privileged minority and in the imposition of political and economic sanctions. On the day following UDI, the Security Council, by a vote of 10 to 0, with France abstaining, condemned the usurpation of power by "a racist settler minority" and called on the United Kingdom to quell the rebellion and on all states to break relations with Rhodesia. Even South Africa and Portugal indicated dismay that their partner in holding the white redoubt of southern Africa had forced the issue in this fashion, refrained from recognizing the rebel regime, and did not officially furnish aid, although vital supplies flowed through and from their countries.

If London and Washington and their partners were inclined to congratulate themselves on the speed with which sanctions were brought into being and to predict the drastic effect which they would have in bringing the rebel government to heel, most of the African states and their supporters protested that what had been done was wholly inadequate and that only intervention by armed force could bring about the downfall of Ian Smith's government and its replacement by a government representative of the African majority. At the extreme, and with

Soviet support, it was charged that the steps which had been taken were only token gestures and that the bonds of "kith and kin" were stronger than any claims of democracy or justice where black men were involved. One of the most grievous consequences of UDI and the reaction to it was the shattering of confidence between black and white, the sense on the part of Africans that they had been betrayed and could count on no effective support even against a regime denounced as treasonable.

As far as the United States was concerned, its connection with Rhodesia was slight as measured by such tangible evidences of involvement as trade and investment. Prior American contact with the country was limited, although it had become somewhat more extensive during the decade 1953-1963, when Salisbury in Southern Rhodesia was the capital and economic headquarters of the Rhodesia-Nyasaland Federation which embraced the rich copper belt of Northern Rhodesia as well. Southern Rhodesia is of no considerable political or strategic interest to the United States, apart from the racial issue which UDI has forced inescapably into the foreground, but the bitter hostility of the African states and peoples to the Rhodesian Front government of Ian Smith makes it impossible to stand aloof.

In a variety of ways the Rhodesian problem is unique. The white population of about 220,000 has been able to maintain and, indeed, since the end of the Federation, to tighten its complete control over the government and economy of the country, allowing no effective participation by the African population of 4 million; yet the trend in recent years had been away from, rather than toward, a policy of apartheid on the South African model. Some of the barriers of segregation and discrimination were dropped in the course of the last decade, including the allocation under the constitution of 1961 of what amounted to fifteen seats for Africans in a parliament with sixty-five members. Although they were not demarcated in racial terms, these fifteen were elected under a separate and less stringent franchise. A great distance remained to be traveled, however, before any approximation of full racial integration could have been achieved.[17]

Once it became evident in 1962-1963 that Britain was prepared to yield to African demands for the breakup of the Federation, the opposition of the Europeans to any move in the direction of majority rule ominously hardened. Thousands of Africans associated with the nationalist movement have been jailed, restricted, or driven into exile. The Congo's troubles are pointed out as lending substance to white fears of an African take-over, as are upheavals and military coups in other parts

[17] Only two items will be cited: Under the Southern Rhodesian Land Apportionment Act, about 48 million acres of land were allotted to the thousands of Europeans and 42 million to the millions of Africans. For a full discussion of land problems, see Montague Yudelman, *Africans on the Land* (Cambridge, Mass.: Harvard University, 1964). Michael Faber calculated that in 1959 the Europeans in Southern Rhodesia had an income per head of £614 a year, as contrasted with £25/4 for the Africans. The expenditure for each European school child by the Federation, which had responsibility for European education, was 26 times that of Southern Rhodesia for each African school child. ("The Distribution of Income Between Racial Groups in Southern Rhodesia," *Race*. May, 1961, pp. 41, 44.)

of Africa, but the relatively good racial relations which have been maintained under African rule in neighboring Zambia and nearby Kenya are usually passed by in silence.

When Northern Rhodesia achieved independence in 1964 under the name of Zambia, and Nyasaland as Malawi, Southern Rhodesia became a key link in the chain guarding white southern Africa, forming its northern bulwark together with Angola and Mozambique. Southern Rhodesia's long frontier with Zambia exposes it to the great block of independent African states to the north, but for the rest it is presently well-cushioned against external subversive contact and serves to bar any direct black African access to South Africa.

On the central point of the determination of the white oligarchy to cling to power, Rhodesia agrees with its white-dominated neighbors, but it differs from them on a number of other important issues. Friendly relations between Rhodesia and the Portuguese territories are important because Rhodesia is landlocked and secures its most direct access to the sea through Mozambique, but differences in style and level of development and, more particularly, in the fundamental question of race relations are great. On the racial score, Rhodesia stands somewhere between South Africa and Portugal, although it is markedly closer to the practice of apartheid than to the Portuguese readiness to assume that racial differences are of less consequence than difference in levels of civilization.

The most logical ally for white Rhodesia in an unfriendly world is undoubtedly South Africa, with which it shares not only a common frontier but many aspects of a common situation and outlook as well, but an informal alliance or covert agreement to collaborate is as intimate an association between the two as either now desires. Both countries are already in serious international trouble, which closer linkage between them would be likely to intensify. The dominant white majority in Rhodesia, much of it South African in origin, has welcomed the crucial support which has come from South Africa since UDI, but any merger with South Africa would impair Rhodesia's identity and force the adoption of a much tighter apartheid system than now exists. On the South African side, while it is unquestionably important to have buffer states between it and independent black Africa to the north, the incorporation of Rhodesia is undesirable because it would mean the addition of millions of Africans and a relatively small number of whites, the bulk of whom are English-speaking. Furthermore, it would involve complicating the already difficult South African position by linking South Africa with a rebel regime denounced by the United Nations. Sanctions have, however, forced a greater Rhodesian dependence on South Africa, and the latter, while officially holding aloof, has demonstrated its readiness to aid its neighboring white regime. How far South Africa will be prepared to go to preserve Rhodesia as an independent white state may well depend on the way in which the issue is posed. South Africa has an evident stake in seeing sanctions against Rhodesia fail since their success would encourage similar action against herself; and mandatory sanctions, perhaps enforced against South Africa as a main channel of supply for Rhodesia, could bring a decision to embrace the white Rhodesian cause more openly. In the opening rounds South Africa played its hand more cautiously.

The must unusual and most disputed feature of all is the nature of the relationship with Great Britain. The nub of the matter is contained in the self-contradictory description of the country as a self-governing colony. In 1923 the white settlers voted against joining South Africa and in favor of responsible government as a British colony, the far more numerous Africans being, of course, left wholly out. From that time forward, the sphere of Rhodesian self-government was confirmed and expanded. Britain retained an ultimate but shadowy sovereignty, a virtually unused right to protect the African population against discriminatory legislation, and the management of foreign affairs. By what came to be well-established constitutional conventions, London undertook no interference in the domestic affairs of the country. The British view of the relationship was firmly stated by Duncan Sandys, Secretary of State for Commonwealth Relations and Colonies, in the House of Commons on November 15, 1963:

> Southern Rhodesia has for over forty years enjoyed complete internal self-government. Up to the creation of the Federation she was responsible for her own defense . . . I hope that those outside who always tell us that we ought to interfere, and do this or that in Southern Rhodesia, will realize that there is not a single official or soldier in Southern Rhodesia responsible to the British Government. We have long accepted the principle that Parliament at Westminster does not legislate for Southern Rhodesia except at its request.[18]

The British position in fact rested on two contradictory propositions which were so designed as to give Britain the largest possible measure of freedom. On one side, London insisted that since Rhodesia was self-governing, Britain was exempted from any obligation to the UN under Chapter XI; but, on the other side, since Rhodesia was still a colony and could achieve independence only by a grant of Parliament, Britain retained responsibility for it and rejected any UN action in relation to it as an improper intervention in the domestic affairs of a member state. In the UN, however, the anti-colonialists were inclined to take a reverse stand and to contend that since Rhodesia was a colony, the metropole must possess the authority and machinery to keep it in line. If the Queen commanded the power to abrogate the constitution in Guiana and Aden, did she not also command it in Rhodesia? Over strong British objection, which was generally supported by the United States, in 1962 and thereafter both the General Assembly and its committee to implement the 1960 declaration on colonial independence adopted a series of resolutions which rested on a double denial that Rhodesia was self-governing and therefore not within UN jurisdiction and that Britain could not exercise effective control. Among other things, Britain was requested to call a broadly representative conference to draw up a con-

[18] From British Information Services, New York, T. 47 (November 15, 1963), pp. 7-8.

stitution which would "ensure the rights of the majority of the people, on the basis of 'one man, one vote.'"[19]

The pressure on the British was intensified in the UN as fears grew that the breakup of the Federation would mean a strengthening of the white minority. In September, 1963, the issue went to the Security Council which adopted a resolution, inviting Britain not to transfer any powers of sovereignty to Southern Rhodesia until the latter had a government fully representative of all its inhabitants, not to hand over to it federal armed forces and aircraft, and to seek independence for the colony on the basis of equality for all its people.[20] The vote on this resolution was 8 to 1, the United States and France characteristically abstaining, but Britain exercised the third veto in its history to kill it. The question was then moved to the General Assembly where a similar resolution was adopted by a vote of 90 to 2 with 13 abstentions, again including the United States and France. As before, Britain refused to participate on the ground that the UN lacked competence to intervene in Southern Rhodesia's affairs. By agreeing to the turning over to Rhodesia of armed forces previously assigned to the Federation, Britain opened herself to the later charge that she was responsible for Rhodesia's military strength which gravely complicated possible armed action against the rebel government.

Since 1963 Rhodesia has been kept under constant surveillance by one or another UN body; and a stream of resolutions, on which the United States habitually abstained, poured out, but the UN was powerless to do much more than indicate the extent of world disapproval of rule by a white minority and to censure Britain.

As was to be expected, the Labour Party took a somewhat stronger line on the Rhodesian question than the Conservatives. Shortly after taking office, Prime Minister Harold Wilson on October 27, 1964, presumably after consultation with Washington, issued a stern warning as to the consequences of a Rhodesian resort to UDI, denouncing it in advance as an open act of defiance and rebellion which would have no constitutional effect. In short, he declared:

> an illegal declaration of independence in Southern Rhodesia would bring to an end relationships between her and Britain; would cut her off from the rest of the Commonwealth, from most foreign Governments, and from international organizations; would inflict disastrous economic damage upon her; and would leave her isolated and virtually friendless in a largely hostile continent.[21]

[19] Resolution 1747 (XVI) adopted on June 26, 1962 by the Assembly, 73 to 1 (South Africa) with 27 abstentions including the United States. Britain declined to participate in the vote.

[20] President Nkrumah of Ghana held that by the agreement establishing the Federation in 1953, a number of important powers had been transferred from Southern Rhodesia to the federal government, and that the British Parliament was entitled, on the demise of the Federation, to withhold the retransfer of these powers to Southern Rhodesia until such time as it changed its ways in dealing with its African population. See the summary of a note presented by Ghana to Great Britain, *Ghana Today* (London), July 17, 1963.

[21] From British Information Services, New York, T. 38 (October 27, 1964).

On the following day an official American statement gave full support to the Prime Minister's warning and welcomed his insistence that Britain would not sanction independence until satisfied that the people had been allowed full exercise of self-determination.[22] Earlier, as the signs of the impending Rhodesian UDI ominously multiplied, the United States, promising that it would take the necessary concrete steps to halt Rhodesian action, for the first time voted in the General Assembly for a resolution condemning any Rhodesian attempt to seize independence by illegal means and calling on Britain to take all possible measures to block such a move. The resolution carried by a vote of 107 in favor, with only France and Portugal in opposition, but Britain again did not participate in the vote on the ground that Rhodesia was a British and not a UN responsibility. A much more divided vote, however, was accorded an elaborate assembly resolution of November 5 which pointed out increasing cooperation among Southern Rhodesia, South Africa, and Portugal "to perpetuate racist minority rule" and in its most controversial passage called upon Britain to employ all necessary measures, including military force. On this occasion only 82 states voted in favor while the United States joined 8 others in opposition and 18 abstained. As usual, Britain did not participate.

After much anguished negotiation and a flurry of flights between London and Salisbury, the Rhodesian Prime Minister decided to take the final plunge on November 11, 1965, citing in his support ringing passages from the American Declaration of Independence but signally refraining from any assertion that men are created equal or that governments derive their just powers from the consent of the governed.

Britain, the United States, and the UN swung into immediate action. The major British step was the imposition of a number of economic sanctions, including expulsion from the sterling area, the suspension of preferential treatment as a Commonwealth member, the ending of tobacco and sugar purchases, the freezing of Rhodesian funds, and other similar measures. In mid-December an oil embargo was added, directly after a visit by Prime Minister Wilson to President Johnson and in accord with a compromise Security Council resolution of November 20 which urged all states to cut off the shipment of oil and petroleum products to Rhodesia, to end all economic relations with the country, and ban the supplying of arms and ammunition.

Washington acknowledged from the outset that "Britain as the sovereign power in Southern Rhodesia, has the primary responsibility for halting the rebellion in its colony," [23] but at the same time it worked to strengthen the British hand and bolster its resolve. The weakness of the American position in relation to Rhodesia was summed up by one authority in the estimate that "America's direct economic and military interest is infinitesimal and its political and economic influence not much

[22] *The New York Times,* October 29, 1964.
[23] Address by Assistant Secretary of State G. Mennen Williams, December 16, 1965, Department of State Press Release, No. 291.

greater." [24] However slight its direct concern, the United States acted speedily, recalling its Consul-General and joining in partial economic sanctions, including backing for the oil embargo. As early as November 12, Ambassador Goldberg informed the Security Council of the American conviction that self-determination must apply to all the people of Southern Rhodesia and that the rebellion should be brought to an end and majority rule established. The United States also joined Britain in an airlift and other measures to ease the hardships which sanctions inescapably inflicted on Zambia because of that country's dependence on Rhodesia for oil and many other products and for the export of its copper.

The African states took both the prospect and the actuality of Rhodesia's UDI with intense seriousness and were scornful of Britain's claim of inability to prevent it or take all-out action against it. An OAU summit meeting at Accra in October, 1965 asked Britain to suspend the 1961 constitution and take over the administration of the territory by force, if need be. Declaring UDI to be "one of the great political crimes of history," Haile Selassie opened on December 3 a meeting of the OAU Council of Ministers which called for an all-embracing range of sanctions and for preparations for the possible use of force. In an ill-considered move, the council also voted that diplomatic relations with Britain should be broken if she had not crushed the Rhodesian revolt by December 15, of which there was no prospect whatsoever.[25] This pledge was in fact honored by only nine states of which two, Tanzania and Ghana, were Commonwealth members.

Early in 1966, seeing Southern Rhodesia's collapse as a matter of weeks rather than months, the British Prime Minister remained optimistic about the outcome and continued to reject the use of force, but sanctions failed either to bring the Rhodesian government down or to lead it to seek negotiations which would end white minority rule. In order to close one dangerous loophole, the British appealed to the Security Council in April, 1966 to adopt measures which would enable them to prevent the arrival of oil by tanker at Beira, Mozambique, presumed to be destined to move by pipeline to Rhodesia. On April 9, by a vote of 10 to 0, but with 5 abstentions including France and the USSR, a resolution was adopted which held that the situation constituted a threat to the peace and called upon Britain to prevent the arrival of such vessels at Beira by force if necessary. The efforts of African members of the Security Council, backed by the Soviet Union, to call upon Britain to use armed force to make sanctions effective and to bring down the Smith regime were defeated when 8 members of the Council, including the United States, abstained. On December 16, however, the Security Council, for the first time in history, voted mandatory sanctions which called upon all UN members to prevent purchase or shipment of 12 major Rhodesian products, and forbade the supply of oil and oil products to Rhodesia. The United States joined Britain in voting for this resolution; France and the USSR abstained. Washington moved to secure its

[24] Waldemar A. Nielsen, *African Battleline: American Policy Choices in Southern Africa* (New York: Harper, 1965), p. 55.
[25] *The New York Times,* December 4, 1965.

enforcement as far as Americans were concerned, but the African states regarded it as a wholly inadequate, evasive attack upon the rebel white government that they wanted overthrown by force.

The failure to force an overturn in Salisbury brought all the resentments of colonialism and the frustrations of independence bitterly to the surface, including awareness of African impotence to take decisive action. The heart of the matter was the contention that Britain and the others were prepared to act with all the stops out when white men were in danger, but that "natives" could not expect the same solicitous protection. London could send its armed forces to such colonies as Aden and Guiana and to Egypt in the Suez crisis, the United States could ferry Belgian paratroopers to Stanleyville and intervene elsewhere, and the French could fight Algerian rebels for years, but the use of force against British "kith and kin" in Rhodesia was excluded. As Alex Quaison-Sackey, Foreign Minister of Ghana, put it in the Security Council, Britain would use its troops against colonial subjects if their skin were black or brown, but "the blood of white Rhodesian rebels is too sacred to be shed in the interests of African majority rule." The representative of the Ivory Coast protested that the African nationalist leaders were being held as hostages by the white Rhodesians, and he asked whether the drama of Stanleyville would now be followed by that of Salisbury, with the British acting to save black hostages held by white rebels.[26] With scorn the question was posed as to whether Imperial Britain had fallen so low as to be unable to meet the challenge of treason and rebellion thrown in its face by the white colonists.

A year after UDI, Ian Smith had not fallen, and the British Prime Minister had shown his readiness to negotiate with him despite vigorous earlier protestations to the contrary. Rhodesia retained some of its markets, and supplies flowed into it from a variety of sources. The United States, while it instituted a comprehensive embargo on arms and military equipment and on the shipment of petroleum products from this country, did not cut off all trade. Under existing legislation the American government had authority to control exports to Rhodesia, but could control imports only when the Security Council had voted for mandatory sanctions under Article 41 of the Charter. In 1964, American exports to Rhodesia totaled $21 million and American imports $11 million. It became apparent in the first year after UDI that voluntary compliance by American importers with Washington's request to stop the purchase of Rhodesian products could not be counted on to halt the trade. In particular, the American government had asked American importers of Rhodesian chromite and all tobacco trading companies to comply with the British Orders in Council prohibiting the export from Rhodesia of chromite and tobacco. All exports to Rhodesia were placed under license, and the policy was adopted of denying all license applications except for certain foodstuffs, educational material, and goods of a humanitarian or religious nature. The American sugar quotas for Rhodesia for 1965 and 1966 were suspended, and private travel was discouraged.

[26] For a summary of the Security Council debate, see *UN Monthly Chronicle*, II, No. 11 (December, 1965), 14-26. Several speakers held that it was the decision of the British not to use force which emboldened Ian Smith to issue his UDI.

Although there were dissidents, moderates, and extremists on both sides, the line was being drawn with increasing sharpness between those who hoped that patient nonviolent measures would turn the trick and those who believed that only force could bring down an intolerable regime. A strong case, to which Africans were understandably disinclined to listen, could be made against the desirability and probable efficacy of the use of force; but who could tell what would have happened if at the moment of Smith's UDI, Britain had undertaken resolute military intervention? Would the Rhodesian forces have remained loyal to the Crown, or would the British troops have refused to fire on their white opponents? Once the first days were passed, the most likely occasion for British, or conceivably UN, intervention would be provided by a breakdown of law and order in Rhodesia, justifying military measures as a police action rather than as a punitive move, but the never very powerful nationalist forces within the country, their leaders jailed, rusticated, or exiled, remained quiescent on the whole.

Much of the source of African grievance can be laid bare in a single statistic cited by President Nyerere of Tanzania in refutation of the Rhodesian government's claim that it gives equal opportunity to all men in terms of their abilities, regardless of race. The franchise, it is true, is determined not by race but by income and education; but in 1963 the European population of 220,000 sent 19,898 of its own children (for whom education is compulsory between ages 7 and 15) to secondary schools, while the African population of 4 million had only 7,045 children in such schools. With many Africans, Nyerere suggested that, "despite legality and despite the protestations of belief in human equality, the domination of a white minority over blacks is acceptable to the West . . . Free Africa is now waiting with some impatience, to see whether the West really intends to stand on the side of human equality and human freedom." [27]

SOUTH AFRICA

The Republic of South Africa is on all counts the country which is the most difficult to fit into an anti-colonialist world dedicated by the Charter of the UN to respect for human rights and fundamental freedoms for all "without distinction as to race, sex, language, or religion." With the doctrine of apartheid as its guiding star, South Africa is a society uniquely dedicated to the principle of distinctions of race as the basis of its existence. The separation of race from race and the maintenance of the purity and supremacy of the white race are the foundations of the system which the Afrikaner-dominated South African government has brought into being. It can be a matter of no surprise that South

[27] Julius K. Nyerere, "Rhodesia in the Context of Southern Africa," *Foreign Affairs,* 44, No. 3 (April, 1966), 386. A very different view was put forward by Prime Minister Wilson in a speech to the Parliamentary Labour Party on June 15, 1966: "What we have done in Rhodesia is not only to assert the rule of law but to prevent the U.N. and indeed the whole world splitting down the middle in the greatest and most dangerous divide you can have in this century, a division based not on ideology but on color and race which would make all existing divisions . . . look trivial and outdated." (*British Record,* New York, June 23, 1966.)

Africa has been more frequently and more consistently censured by the UN than any other country, that it is the country on which the independent African states look with the greatest abhorrence, and that it is here, rather than anywhere else in Africa, that the United States is likely to be confronted by the gravest decisions and the most threatening conflicts.

Apartheid has met with almost universal denunciation. Indeed, a recent American study asserts that with the exception of South Africa itself, every government in the world has declared it to be wrong, undesirable, and at odds with international standards of human rights and justice.[28] Many of those who have attacked apartheid have used far more vigorous language; and even the delegate from Great Britain, still presumably South Africa's closest friend among the Powers, attacked it in a General Assembly committee in 1962 as "morally abominable, intellectually grotesque, and spiritually indefensible."

Primarily for foreign consumption, but also for the squeamish and idealists at home, South Africa has devised a formulation of apartheid which is not without a certain seductive appeal when it is divorced from the harsh reality of present-day South African life. This version rests upon the proposition that the races of man differ so profoundly from each other that each should be given an opportunity to develop separately and thus achieve its distinctive cultural destiny. In essence this is a radical translation to the African scene of the now discredited American principle of "separate but equal" as the guideline for race relations, and it has as little likelihood of furnishing a satisfactory solution in Africa as it had in the United States. From this racial starting point, it follows that South Africa does not, and should not, constitute a single nation but that it contains a number of distinct nations, including several Bantu peoples, each of which deserves an autonomous territory of its own. These are the so-called Bantustans, of which only one, the Transkei, has so far been brought into being as a subordinate African political system to which distant hope is held out of self-government and association on more equal terms with white South Africa. The emphasis which apartheid has placed on the tribal distinctions within the African community is counted on to fragment the opposition to white supremacy, but it is doubtful that the momentum of the swing away from tribalism generated by white rule can now be reversed, particularly since the modern sectors of the economy are still drawing African labor away from the tribal reserves. Apartheid might be portrayed as a fulfillment of the principle of self-determination, but not if the element of consent plays a role, since only the white minority has been consulted as to whether it wants the kind of self-determination thrust upon all South Africans.

The fatal flaw in apartheid is that its prime motivating force is the

[28] Amelia C. Leiss and Vernon McKay in *Apartheid and United Nations Collective Measures*, ed. Amelia C. Leiss (New York: Carnegie Endowment for International Peace, 1965), p. 5. Waldemar A. Nielsen comments in *African Battleline* (New York: Harper, 1965), p. 64: "Today, even though diplomatic and economic relationships with South Africa are generally maintained, its moral isolation from the world community is virtually total. Never in modern times, and perhaps never in history—not even in the case of Hitler Germany or Stalinist Russia—has a government brought down upon itself so unanimously the moral disapproval of the world."

desire of the white community, led by the Afrikaner majority, to hold on to its privileged position, to maintain its separate identity, and to secure to itself the benefits flowing from the highly productive society which it has created with the aid of cheap African labor. These are goals which the governing Nationalist Party is prepared to pursue with ruthless zeal, as experience has amply demonstrated. Probably no scheme of apartheid could have succeeded in South Africa, no matter how equitably, generously, and idealistically conceived and administered. Certainly ultimate failure is inevitable when some 3,500,000 whites hold the whiphand over more than 12,000,000 Africans, 1,800,000 Coloreds (persons of mixed blood), and 500,000 Indians. The true nature of the relationship between white and black South Africans is vividly illuminated by two figures which are in good part no more than two sides of the same South African coin. The minority white community has reserved to itself 87 per cent of the land of South Africa, while the African majority is endowed with the remaining 13 per cent. This gross imbalance renders incredible the idea that Africans might be persuaded to settle for the reserves or Bantustans into which they are now being crowded. The second figure, showing the reverse of the coin, reveals that only some 40 per cent of the African population is found in the "Bantu homelands," and that despite apartheid the remaining 60 per cent live and labor in the white domain, more or less evenly divided between urban and rural areas. In these areas they have no status as of right and are at the disposition of the white authorities who do not accept them as even potential members of a single South African society.

Since the African leaders have been jailed, exiled, or otherwise silenced, it is difficult to get an accurate picture of the African reaction, but the constant tightening of the official security measures presumably reflects the pressure from below. The transformation of South Africa into a police state is already far advanced, although both the judiciary and the press continue to have a surprising degree of freedom. The government is equipped with extraordinary powers, with a large, well-organized and well-equipped police force and with a network of informers black as well as white, which have crippled all efforts to construct opposition political movements. The military forces have expanded to the point where internal security and defense expenditures have increased fourfold since 1960 and now absorb more than a quarter of the budget. The ruling circles evidently regard their regime as being under severe attack; but the preparations which they have taken leave no doubt that both internal and external opponents of the regime face a grim struggle.

The direct American concern with South Africa is somewhat greater than with most of the rest of the continent, but it does not begin to measure up to that of the British, whose deep involvement inevitably influences American policy. Politically and strategically, in the ever-present setting of the Cold War, South Africa is an ardently anti-Communist power whose position at the southern extremity of Africa still gives it potential strategic importance. If prime significance is attached to the Communist issue, then it may well seem folly to take any steps which endanger the present South African government, although it is also arguable that its racist practices are sure to act as a major stimulant to Communism at home and abroad. The spokesmen for the existing regime make much of the stability and prosperity of South Africa as contrasted with the rest of Africa's independent states and stress the relative material well-being and educational advance of its African population. In May, 1962, Prime Minister Verwoerd expressed somewhat scornful doubt that the United States would cut itself off from the benefits which it derived from its relations with South Africa and would allow the country to "be thrown to the wolves or be swallowed up by the fluctuating ideological streams which, inspired partly by communism, flow across Africa, rather than accept her as being, by nature, a safe and sure and permanent friend." [29]

It is in this latter light that American businessmen and investors have been inclined to view South Africa. Thus, General Norstad, billed by the South African Information Service in May, 1965 as "retired NATO supreme commander and now a top American businessman," coming to South Africa with a big investment blueprint, was quoted as stating that "We have full confidence in South Africa—not only we as individuals but the United States and the American people as well." [30] Such a statement, of course, sharply contradicts the official American position; but it is also noteworthy that while the State Department and American delegates to the UN used strong words about South Africa, the Department of Commerce continued to promote American trade with, and investment in, the country or at least to regard it with benevolent neutrality.

Estimates as to American private investment in South Africa differ widely, but a frequently cited figure is $600 million to $700 million or some 15 per cent of the total foreign investment in the country, while the British investment is estimated to come to more than $2.5 billion, or well over half the total.[31] The South African economy has proved attractive to American investors, and the return on investment has been unusually high. The matter was succinctly put by a correspondent of *The Christian Science Monitor* on December 10, 1965 in answer to a query as to what American interests profit from apartheid:

[29] Cited in *South African Crisis and United States Policy* by Collin Gonze, George M. Houser, and Perry Sturges (New York: American Committee on Africa, 1962), p. 46.

[30] *South African Scope* (New York: Information Service of South Africa, May, 1965), p. 12. He was joined in this statement by Harold Boeschenstein, who was identified as "Chairman of the biggest fiberglass manufacturing organization in the world."

[31] *Survey of Current Business,* Department of Commerce (Washington, September, 1966) states American direct private investment in South Africa to be $528 million in 1965. Much valuable information on economic relations is contained in *United States-South African Relations* (Hearings before the Subcommittee on Africa of the Committee on Foreign Affairs, House of Representatives, 89th Cong., 2nd session, Part 1). See particularly the testimony of Assistant Secretary of State Williams and Assistant Secretary of Commerce Trowbridge on March 1 and 2, 1966. I am indebted to Dr. Sanford D. Greenberg for allowing me to consult his unpublished Harvard doctoral dissertation, submitted in 1965: "United States Policy Toward the Republic of South Africa, 1945-64."

What they are is simply a who's who among corporations on the New York Stock Exchange. All the big names are there as investors operating plants in a booming economy—Ford, General Motors, General Electric, Minnesota Mining, IBM, Standard Oil of California, Borden, Chrysler, Coca-Cola, etc.—over 80 big corporations were recently listed.[32]

It is the customary plea of the concerns undertaking investment in South Africa that their problem is profit and not politics. Whether they appreciate the kind of order and stability which has been imposed or regret the obligatory racial discrimination, their activities in fact serve to bolster the Natonalist government and therefore its universally condemned system of apartheid. The unusual rate of profit which has attracted them to the country derives, at least in part, from the low wages of African workers which are inherent in the system. Since new investment from both the United States and Great Britain has been slight or nonexistent in recent years, it is this high return which has made the expansion of investment possible through the plowing back of profits.

American investment in South Africa comes to just over 1 per cent of total American foreign investment, and American trade with South Africa represents approximately the same percentage of total American foreign trade. In 1963 the value of American exports to South Africa was $276 million while the imports from South Africa came to $259 million. The British share in South African trade has been more than double the American, and the more vulnerable British economy, 5 per cent of whose exports go to South Africa, is far more dependent on this trade and the return from its investment than is the United States.[33] In terms of the magnitude both of British investment in the country and of the purchase of British goods, South Africa stands fourth among the countries of the world. The great bulk of both British and American exports to South Africa falls in the category of manufactured goods: machinery and vehicles, textiles, and chemicals; while the imports, in addition to gold, are primarily minerals and other raw materials and foodstuffs.

In most summary terms it may be said that the cutting off of all economic intercourse with South Africa, which has become at least a speculative possibility since more and more UN members have called for sanctions, would impose only relatively incidental burdens on the United States. Such a cutting off would, however, seriously impair the British

[32] The correspondent, Earl W. Foell, added that the New Jersey financier, Charles W. Englehard, listed as a director of 23 South African companies, "is also a heavy contributor to the Democratic Party and a friend of President Johnson." Drew Middleton, writing from Johannesburg, stated that there are 247 U.S. companies in South Africa, "most of them profitable and some making profits of 20 per cent on their investments." (*The New York Times*, April 30, 1966.) See the 1966 *United States-South African Relations* hearings, pp. 15-26, for a list of U.S. subsidiaries, affiliates, and branch offices in South Africa.

[33] The UN Secretariat in a report dated Aug. 22, 1966, prepared for the Special Committee on Apartheid, estimated that the earnings of the United Kingdom on its direct investment in South Africa rose from 11 per cent in 1961 to 16 per cent, in 1964, of all its earnings from direct overseas investment. The comparable American figures were 1.4 and 1.7 per cent. (Tables 13 and 15 in UN Doc. A/AC.115/L. 56/Rev. 2.)

economy, which has already suffered heavy losses because of the Rhodesian sanctions. Prime Minister Wilson informed the Commonwealth conference in London in September, 1966, that the cost of the sanctions to Britain had risen to £100 million. A survey of British interests in South Africa undertaken under the auspices of the Royal Institute of International Affairs in 1965 concluded that a total interruption of commerce would cause "the immediate loss of a twentieth of Britain's export trade, the disappearance of a traditional source of supply for a number of items, and the sudden drying up of £60 million a year in foreign exchange." [34] Some 150,000 workers would be thrown out of work; the earnings derived from the trade in gold would dry up; and British shipping, banking, and insurance operations would be hard hit. These are consequences which no British government could lightly face, particularly at a time when balance of payments problems are already grave.

If one looks at the matter from the other side of the fence, it is, of course, evident that South Africa is economically much more dependent on Britain than Britain is on South Africa. About one-third of South Africa's foreign trade is conducted with Great Britain, which also furnishes South Africa a number of important services, but it must be taken into account that any damage inflicted on South Africa might also have serious consequences for Botswana, Lesotho, and Swaziland.

Although the direct American stake in South Africa is not great, for the last two decades the United States has been unavoidably entangled in that country's affairs, in part through the UN where South Africa has been habitually under attack. Three major issues have been involved: the treatment of Indians in South Africa, apartheid, and the relations with Southwest Africa. As the years have gone by, attention has come to be focused more and more on the central theme of apartheid, which also figures in the charges against South African policy toward Southwest Africa, whose problems have occupied much International Court attention.

When the issue of racial conflict in South Africa, which meant apartheid, appeared on the General Assembly docket in 1952, the United States for some years abstained on resolutions attacking it, contending both that the UN was not authorized to intervene in South Africa's domestic affairs and that such intervention was not likely to achieve the desired results. A change came in 1958 as Washington was becoming aware that it could no longer evade the emergence of a new Africa. Then the United States was prepared to accept the Assembly's right to chide South Africa for actions inconsistent with the human rights provisions of the Charter; and, in keeping with its new attack upon its own race problems at home, it specifically expressed its dislike of a society based on segregation and discrimination. On such grounds, it voted for the

---

[34] Dennis Austin, *Britain and South Africa* (London, New York, Toronto: Oxford University, 1966), p. 160. Other estimates of the probable impact of sanctions may be found in *Sanctions Against South Africa*, ed. Ronald Segal (Middlesex, England: Penguin Books, 1964), particularly pp. 167-203; Leiss, *Apartheid and United Nations,* Chap. 6; and the *Report of the Expert Committee Established in Pursuance of Security Council Resolution S/5773* (S/6210).

first time for a resolution which mildly expressed "regret and concern" about South Africa's racial policies.

The next major turn in American policy came as a result of the notorious Sharpeville incident when, on March 21, 1960, the police fired into a crowd of African demonstrators, reportedly killing 67 and wounding 186. This shooting down of Africans caused worldwide consternation and led to an immediate official statement in Washington deploring violence and the tragic loss of life. The Security Council was called into action and adopted a relatively strong resolution, backed by the United States although Britain and France abstained, which deplored South Africa's policies and actions and held that the situation might come to endanger international peace and security.

The coincidence of Sharpeville with the multiplication of African states in the UN led to pressure for stronger action to force South Africa to abandon its racial practices and move with the winds of change which Prime Minister Macmillan had evoked in his speech to the South African Parliament on February 3, 1960. Resolutions of the conventional type, regretting and deploring, were obviously ineffective in inducing South Africa to yield. As a result, the United States now found itself confronted by the necessity of dealing with an increasingly insistent demand for sanctions. As one pamphlet put it.

> It appeared that no sooner had the United States moved to the point where it could, in good conscience, vote for a mildly condemnatory resolution, than the majority of world opinion took another long stride ahead, leaving the U.S. again in the minority, along with the "colonialist" nations.[35]

In 1961 the United States and its associates were able to defeat a resolution calling for sanctions, but in the following year the more intransigent foes of South Africa succeeded in passing a sanctions resolution which requested the breaking off of diplomatic relations and a boycott of South African shipping and aircraft as well as of trade in both directions, specifically including a ban on the export of arms and ammunition. The anti-colonialists mustered 60 votes for this resolution, but the fact that 16 members opposed and 21 abstained indicated how wide a difference of opinion existed. Even more important was the fact that the 16 states which voted against the resolution embraced the leading Western powers, including the United States, Britain, and France, as well as Japan, Canada, Australia, and New Zealand. South Africa's Foreign Minister Eric Louw, took pleasure in pointing out the salient fact that "The nations not supporting sanctions absorb 79.6 per cent of South Africa's exports and send her 63.7 per cent of her imports." [36] Since the resolution was only a recommendation, lacking binding force, it was

---

[35] Gonze, Houser, and Sturges, *South African Crisis,* p. 44.

[36] *A New Course in South Africa* (New York: United Nations, 1964), p. 29. This is the report of the Group of Experts, headed by Alva Myrdal, which was established by the Security Council in resolution S/5471 on December 4, 1963, to examine methods of resolving the South African situation.

idle to expect that in such circumstances it could have much impact on South Africa, and even some of the African states have been accused of not observing its provisions.

The United States had for some years expressed its disapproval of South Africa's course in strong language—in 1962, for example, declaring it to be a policy which could lead to "bloodshed, war, and disaster for all races." On October 19, 1962, it went a step further when Adlai Stevenson informed the General Assembly that the United States was forbidding the sale to the South African government of arms and military equipment which could be used to enforce apartheid either in South Africa or in Southwest Africa. On August 2, 1963, he told the Security Council that the United States expected to stop, before the end of the year, the sale of all military equipment to the South African government apart from the need to honor certain existing contracts, and the British immediately thereafter announced that they would ban all export of arms which could be used to further the policy of apartheid. The setting for these announcements was, however, a futile anti-colonialist effort to obtain Security Council endorsement for a boycott of South Africa which won only five votes. The resolution which finally passed on August 7, 1963, "solemnly calls upon all states" to cease the sale and shipment of arms, ammunition, and military vehicles to South Africa. Nine Council members, including the United States, voted for this resolution, while Britain and France abstained. Stevenson contended that to apply mandatory sanctions would be both bad policy and bad law. The Security Council, he held, was not empowered to apply coercive measures in such a situation, since—although South Africa failed to live up to certain of its Charter obligations—it did not aggressively threaten the peace.

As is true of so much of its African policy, the relations of the United States with South Africa are marked by a cautious gradualism which can either be praised as a sensible and realistic appraisal of the situation or criticized as a refusal to face up to the hard facts of life as Africans and Asians see them. The readiness of the United States to take drastic action against China, Cuba, and other Communist regimes is inevitably contrasted with its scruples and hesitations about doing more than entering verbal and diplomatic protests in other cases. As American critics put it: "The United States presently boycotts and embargoes countries in which over a third of the world's population lives. Yet it has been unwilling to go beyond a ban of arms and ammunition to implement UN resolutions against apartheid." [37]

With almost the sole exception of its prompt hostile reaction to the Sharpeville incident, the United States has followed along well behind the UN majority and has continued on the whole to maintain normal and friendly relations with South Africa, including the presence in South Africa of American satellite tracking facilities. If a number of private American groups and organizations have given valuable aid to Africans within the country and in exile, a number of other Americans and corporations have participated in white South Africa's prosperous economy.

[37] "Partners in Apartheid: United States Policy on South Africa," *Africa Today*, March, 1964, p. 11.

Apartheid-minded South Africans, while pained at American condemnation of their government's policies, have taken comfort from American participation in the Stanleyville paratroop landing and its backing for Tshombe and his white mercenaries as well as from the general unreadiness of the United States to break with their country.

A worsening of relations with South Africa came in the aftermath of the deplorable failure of the International Court in its decision of July 18, 1966, to rule on the substantive issues which had been so long argued before it in the case brought by Ethiopia and Liberia against South African rule in the mandated territory of Southwest Africa. On July 27, the Department of State pointed out the limited nature of the Court's ruling and emphasized that the mandate continued in force, as the Court had affirmed in earlier advisory opinions, and that South Africa remained responsible to the UN for its administration of the territory. A major manifestation of the disaffection aroused by the Court's ruling was a resolution presented to the General Assembly by a number of African and Asian states, which condemned South Africa and called upon the UN itself to take over the administration of Southwest Africa. On October 12, Ambassador Arthur J. Goldberg, speaking for the United States, took the unexpected step of declaring in the Assembly's debate on this resolution that South Africa had forfeited "all right to continue to administer the territory of Southwest Africa," [38] and a fortnight later joined the overwhelming majority of the Assembly in voting for a resolution which asserted that South Africa's mandate was terminated and that Southwest Africa was henceforward a direct responsibility of the UN. The South African Foreign Minister promptly responded that his country would resist with all the power at its disposal any moves which endangered the safety of peoples committed to its care.

That the Africans have legitimate grievances against the usual passivity of the Western attitude toward the fatherland of apartheid and that there are a number of untried ways in which the United States might bring pressure to bear on South Africa should not be allowed to lead without very serious examination to the conclusion that manadatory sanctions would provide the proper answer. It may be that such sanctions will prove to be inescapable if apartheid's evils are to be rooted out, but they would constitute a drastic step whose consequences for the United States, its major allies, and the world at large would surely be very serious. Confronted by the threat of sanctions or other hostile operations, South Africa has done much to improve its ability to stand by itself. The Minister of Defense has declared that the country is practically self-sufficient in armaments production, and the ability to survive an oil embargo seems much greater than a few years ago. Undoubtedly, serious damage could be inflicted on South Africa *if* substantially all countries lived up to the call for sanctions, but this is a condition which can derive little support from the available precedents, including the Rhodesian case. For Britain, the breaking off of economic relations would have such dire implications as to make the adoption of sanctions highly improbable. This would obviously be a matter of great concern for the

[38] *The New York Times,* Oct. 13, 1966.

United States, as would the likelihood that American forces would have to play a major role in imposing a blockade on what might come to be some 3,000 miles of coastline, if the Portuguese territories are added to South and Southwest Africa, in order to make sanctions effective.

Even assuming effective sanctions, one must still entertain doubts as to what the results would be. Would the Nationalists and their supporters cave in under pressure, or would they be driven to a last-ditch resistance; and, if the latter, what kind of South Africa would be left at the end, and who would pick up the pieces? C.W. de Kiewiet has pointed out that "The past decade has given Americans a painful experience in bringing men to compliance with the verdict of even the highest court," adding that it would be hard to expect unanimity in American opinion over involvement in the racial affairs of a distant country.[39]

One of the possibilities which must enter into the calculation is that the United States, hesitating to take decisive steps, might at some point find itself confronted by a coalition of African states, with much of Asia and of the Communist world behind them, for action against South Africa to break the back of apartheid. At this distance it is difficult to see how such a grouping of states could bring very effective pressure to bear upon South Africa, but the mere fact that the United States resorted to neutralist abstention would make its moral and political position difficult and unhappy. The probable result would be to alienate many African countries already bitter over the Rhodesian situation, and push them toward an alignment with the Communist powers.

In the interim, as sanctions are debated and rejected by the United States and its partners, relations between the United States and South Africa become somewhat more difficult, with neither side prepared to seek a showdown with the other.[40] Thus the United States has maintained full diplomatic relations with South Africa but has since 1963 held multiracial receptions at the American Embassy which have been protested and boycotted by the South African government as in violation of the customs of the country; but the United States has sent no Negro Foreign Service officers. The Prime Minister has announced that his government would not permit Negroes to be assigned to the satellite tracking facilities which the United States continues to operate in South Africa, and the American aircraft carrier "Independence" bypassed Capetown when the South African government decreed that no Negroes could be landed from the ship. On both sides, positions have been taken which leave no doubt of sharp opposition in matters of basic policy, but there was a deliberate refusal to spell them out in detail and in public. At least to outward appearance, South Africa remained confident that the United

---

[39] C. W. de Kiewiet, "South Africa's Gamble with History," *Virginia Quarterly Review*, XL, No. 1 (Winter, 1965), 6. Waldemar A. Nielsen concludes his brief and well-balanced analysis of the problem with the assertion that for the United States to adopt any course other than a rejection of mandatory sanctions "would be a violation of its own responsibilities as a world leader and contrary to the interests of its own citizens and of all mankind." (*African Battleline*, p. 86.)

[40] For the following incidents, see *The New York Times*, March 10, June 27-28, July 3, and August 18, 1965.

States, despite verbal attacks, would not abandon the advantages and profits of various kinds it draws from continued friendly intercourse, as it remained confident that Britain would not endanger its larger economic stake and its agreed access to the Simonstown base, north of the Cape of Good Hope, which, London indicated in 1966, Britain was prepared to abandon.

The lesser Rhodesian affair has perplexed statesmen and sharpened racial antagonisms. The far greater South African issue, which might turn into a major catastrophe, was still only gathering its explosive force in the mid-1960's.

7

Conclusion

American policy toward Africa in the era of independence can either be lauded as representing a sane, well-balanced, and responsible course of action, or downgraded as timid, unimaginative, and ill-attuned to African needs and aspirations. Which side of this controversy one chooses to take depends less upon the facts of the case—although which facts are selected may obviously be of crucial significance—than upon the assumptions and expectations from which one sets off.

As the United States played only a slight direct role in promoting the independence of African colonies, so it has generally lagged behind the more dynamic of African leaders who at least on anti-colonial and racial issues could usually carry all or the bulk of Africa with them. A case can be made, indeed, for the proposition that the only extended period during which American policy and African nationalist aspirations were reasonably well in balance was during the first year or so of the Kennedy administration when the African states were still tentatively feeling their way and the United States had taken a leap into more venturesome policies; but radical African nationalism soon left the United States behind again. Although John F. Kennedy's coming to office lent a freshness and new vitality to the American approach to Africa,[1] the special glow imparted to the relationship by President Kennedy left little trace. It was not that Lyndon Johnson had any hostility to Africa, but only that the warm and intimate concern of his predecessor was gone. The appealing

[1] Kennedy's special interest in Africa is well brought out in Arthur M. Schlesinger, Jr.'s, *A Thousand Days*, particularly in Chap. XXI, "Africa, the New Adventure."

special interest which Washington had shown in Africa receded as Africa became again the least considered of the continents; and Africa was soon aware of the change.[2]

Almost all the special circumstances which had made a honeymoon period of African-American relations possible had vanished or largely lost their relevance well before the American entanglement with Tshombe in 1964 which culminated in the shock to African opinion caused by the Stanleyville paratroop landing. At the outset, when only a few states were involved, it seemed not unrealistic to assume that an American program of benevolent cooperation and technical aid could serve across the board to win their approbation, since they all seemed to be headed in the same direction. Americans were generally optimistic about the new African states, expecting them to be friendly, democratic, eager for development, and grateful for American aid. The Africans, for their part, expected the United States to be a major source of good things—material and otherwise—and to serve both as a counterweight to the colonial powers and as a door opening the way to new vistas of a world from which colonialism had largely debarred them. If a small number of Africans were hostile to the United States for doctrinaire reasons or because of experience of American racial practices, the bulk of both leaders and multitudes were friendly and hopeful of closer relations.

As more and more African states came on the scene and their policies became more sharply differentiated, it was increasingly obvious that no single line of American policy could hope to satisfy everybody. "Our purpose and policy is plain," asserted Assistant Secretary of State Williams in 1961, "We want for Africa what the Africans want for themselves";[3] a proposition which was feasible when the Africans appeared to be of one mind but which became problematical when they disagreed among themselves. The cleavage, for example, between the more left-oriented, "progressive" states of the Guinea-Ghana-Mali stripe and the more conservative position of many of the rest forced the United States to pick and choose, thus inevitably disaffecting some and usually precisely those who spoke up most vociferously. Congo-Brazzaville was

---

[2] *Jeune Afrique* (Tunis), August, 1965, gave the results of a poll which asked over 7,000 persons from French-speaking African states at home and abroad: "Who is the non-African statesman who has in recent years shown the most understanding and friendship for the non-committed nations?" The outcome was: de Gaulle 4,383, Tito 860, Kennedy 808, Chou En-lai 408, Khrushchev 134, Johnson 56, Mao 34, Castro 20. Another question asked which non-African country is the best friend of the Africans and the underdeveloped peoples. The leading countries were ranked as follows:

	Maghreb	Black Africa	Foreign countries	Total
France	1,102	1,716	144	2,962
China	950	485	89	1,524
Yugoslavia	1,181	93	47	1,321
USSR	422	72	26	520
U.S.	204	148	—	352

[3] See *The Christian Science Monitor* (Boston), October 26, 1961.

unlikely to view what went on in Leopoldville across the river in the same fashion as Ethiopia or Nigeria, and Southern Rhodesia's neighbors, Zambia and Malawi, differing between themselves, were highly likely to differ from Senegal or Uganda in their reaction to Rhodesian developments. Nor was this only a question as between states, since the same issues in varying degrees divided the citizenry within many of the African countries. Thus in Nigeria a sizeable proportion of the politically-minded in the southern regions repudiated the conservatism of the Northern-dominated government in Lagos, an attitude which played at least a subsidiary role in the military coup of January, 1966, engineered in the first instance primarily by Ibo officers. Ghana's corresponding coup in the succeeding month represented a take-over by moderate or conservative forces which repudiated Nkrumah's radicalism.

It also became more and more evident that some of the policies which Africans advocated with growing intransigence by no means necessarily laid out courses of action which the United States was prepared to pursue. Where African leaders passionately sought drastic and immediate action, the United States was inclined to counsel caution and slow motion. Most frequently the concrete issues which were involved in such controversies concerned either the Congo or the so-called white redoubt of southern Africa; but the Africans noted with shocked dismay that when the United States itself undertook drastic action it was not in Angola or South Africa, but to rescue white hostages in the Congo.

African-American relations have been rendered more difficult and given the appearance of being more intractable than they actually are by the tendency on both sides to clothe in high moral terms the positions taken on major issues. Africa's spokesmen are inclined to attribute moral validity only to their own strongly-held views on colonial and racial matters or the need for development, and to blame anything which goes wrong on the imperialists. The corresponding American touchstone is the degree and depth of anti-Communist commitment, with the implication that those who give other questions higher priority, as virtually all Africans do, are either blind or dupes of the archenemy.

These are, of course, in some measure caricatures of American and African positions, but they possess enough of reality to point up homely truths. As the United States has been inclined to look under the bed for Communists, so Africans have clung to the illusion of a natural harmony of African interests, if the imperialists will only leave them alone. Thus Nkrumah wanted all tribalism cast out of Ghana's national life: "We are all Africans and peoples of African descent, and we shall not allow the imperialist plotters and intriguers to separate us from each other for their own advantage." [4] In the same vein, Julius Nyerere, pleading for pan-Africanism, asserted that "We must use African national states as an instrument for the unification of Africa, and not allow our enemies to use them as tools for dividing Africa." [5] What is missing is recognition that African peoples and states, like those everywhere in the world, are

[4] Kwame Nkrumah, *I Speak of Freedom* (New York: Praeger, 1961), p. 168.

[5] Julius K. Nyerere, *The Second Scramble*. Speech before a World Association of Youth Seminar, Dar es Salaam, 1961.

quite capable of falling out among themselves without the need of some alien evil genius to destroy their harmony, and that outsiders may disagree with Africans without necessarily being enemies.

This is not intended to deny that anyone who is so inclined, as are numbers of Asians and Africans, can produce documented evidence to support the charge that the imperialists remain unreconciled to the successes of the colonial liberation movement. Even leaving aside the more subtle manipulations of neo-colonialism, the anti-imperialists can point to a long series of overt events, such as the Anglo-French attack on Egypt in the Suez crisis, the French colonial wars in Indochina and Algeria, the violent clash between France and Tunisia in 1961 over the naval base at Bizerte, and the armed intervention of France in Gabon in 1964 to rescue President Leon Mba from overthrow, the escalating American war in Vietnam and the affairs of Cuba and the Dominican Republic, and the Stanleyville paratroop operation. These are all matters which are clear on the record. How much weight should they be given, particularly when balanced against the equally plain fact that hundreds of millions of colonial peoples have won or been conceded their freedom? Imperialism of the old style is far nearer to being dead than its critics and its enemies often give it credit for being.

As a general rule, it is more realistic to assume that disagreements between African countries or between them and the United States are not ordinarily caused by sinister alien forces but rather reflect significant differences in the position of states and in their estimate as to how best to safeguard and promote their interests. It is folly to think that in a continent as vast and diverse as Africa all peoples would see eye to eye or that serious divergences would not from time to time divide African states from a country as remote and differently situated as the United States. Even with full American sympathy and good will for Africa, there is no reason to assume that the American national interest will necessarily coincide with the African interest, although the potential range of coincidence seems great.

DISINTEREST OR INDIFFERENCE?

The United States can still in large part follow a disinterested policy in relation to Africa in the sense that its specific interests continue to be relatively slight and that it is still not closely identified with particular African countries. Since the American economic interest is of no outstanding significance, amounting for the entire continent to less than 5 per cent of the total American foreign trade and investment, any interpretation of American policy which derives primarily from economic factors has a ring of improbability to it; nor is there reason to believe that the drive of American economic interests to establish themselves in Africa is so great and persuasive as to exercise a dominant influence on American policy.

It is consistent with both the basic American policy of anti-communism and other American purposes more congenial to the Africans that the

United States should follow policies which may legitimately be characterized as benevolent. By fortunate accident it happens that the American national interest, as a general proposition, is served by African economic, social, and political development, by moves designed to promote African collaboration and unity, and by the maintenance of peace in the continent—all, of course, to be carried forward under non-communist auspices. To anyone partial to the left-wing charges that the United States is the archimperialist, seeking only to dominate Africa in order to exploit it more fully, such a statement as this must seem either ridiculously naïve or wantonly corrupt; and yet it is arguable that the primary American sin in Africa is not that it has so grossly intervened in African affairs but that it has so often regarded Africa as one of its peripheral concerns to which it need pay little consecutive attention. If American intentions are good, and even reasonably honorable, it is also true that they bear low priority and have little steam behind them. African development is seen as desirable on all counts, but it is not a matter to which major American resources are currently to be devoted.

As Arnold Rivkin has put it, "our unwillingness to take more initiative in Africa is the more remarkable because it is the one area in the world in which the United States has more freedom of action and fewer constraints on its foreign-policy making than in any other."[6] Regrettably, a disinterested policy can be an indifferent one as well.

Furthermore, the disinterested character of American policy toward Africa ensures neither that that policy will be wise nor that it will fit in with what the Africans see as their interests. It is evident that the United States has many interests which do not directly concern Africa, and inevitably some of them will run counter to African desires. For the most part, to be sure, Washington can follow policies in relation to Africa which are explicitly framed to deal with African problems and needs, but from time to time conflicts of interest prove unavoidable. Operationally, in Washington terms, the issue has often posed itself in contrary courses of action advocated by the African, as opposed to the European, desks in the State Department, forcing decision at a higher level where the concerns of Africa are only one element, and sometimes only a negligible element, in the total picture. Certainly it is true that there is no reason why the European desks should take priority on matters primarily concerning Africa, but it is equally true that the African interest must occasionally give way.

A case can be made for the proposition that in many, perhaps in most, spheres there is no occasion for any sharp divergence of interest between the United States and African countries, but African-American relations are bound to be rendered difficult and touchy by the basic contrast between American wealth, power, advancement, and attachment to private enterprise on one side and African poverty, weakness, backwardness, and attachment to socialism on the other. More particular sources of actual or potential disagreement are not hard to identify.

[6] Arnold Rivkin, "Lost Goals in Africa," *Foreign Affairs,* XLIV, No. 1 (October, 1965), p. 116.

Honest differences of opinion can easily arise as to the effectiveness or feasibility of particular courses of action: e.g., assuming agreement on the goal of ridding South Africa of apartheid, can sanctions be successfully invoked to that end, and if so, what kind of sanctions, how enforced, etc.? Moving upward on the scale, in 1964 the United States saw as the most pressing need in the Congo steps to put an end to disorder, to get rid of the rebels, to dispose of the Communist threat, and to rescue the hostages, while to many Africans no action was tolerable which involved collaboration with Tshombe and his white mercenaries. At the highest level, the Assistant Secretary of State for African Affairs, Joseph C. Satterthwaite, in 1960, shortly before the Sharpeville incident, raised before the Senate Foreign Relations Committee with obvious reference to South Africa the problem as to what a government can do to counter racialism in another friendly country "whose foreign policies at least strongly support the United States in the overriding issues of our times." [7] Here the paramount question is flatly posed. For Washington the overriding issues center about the menace of communism; for most Africans this is an irrelevance which blocks attention to the *real* overriding issues which are colonialism, racialism, and underdevelopment.

In sum, Africa has risen greatly in the American scheme of things in the last decade, but it must still inevitably compete with other parts of the world which the United States views with greater and more continuous concern. The NATO alliance, despite its present disarray, remains the cornerstone of American foreign policy, and Britain remains America's principal ally. In what may come to be the most urgent case of all, is it conceivable that the United States should join in the imposition of sanctions on South Africa without weighing most gravely the probable effects on British economic and political stability? Or could Washington allow itself to become committed to drastic action of any kind in Africa while the Vietnam war continued to escalate?

THE UNITED STATES AND AFRICAN GOVERNMENTS

The inner logic of anti-communism as a central feature of American policy presents the United States with a dilemma. The traditional American assumption is that the United States consorts most happily with governments of a liberal democratic persuasion, but the anti-communism of conservative or reactionary regimes makes them immediately attractive and congenial while those of the liberal left are inevitably somewhat suspect. To the argument that reactionary regimes, by blocking legitimate access to change, breed more Communists than they get rid of, the official attitude appears often to be that an anti-communist in the hand is worth two in the bush.

In Africa, liberal democratic governments have been hard to find since with only rare exceptions the successors to the colonial regimes moved

[7] Cited by Sanford D. Greenberg, "United States Policy Toward the Republic of South Africa," p. 12. Mr. Satterthwaite was shortly to become the American Ambassador to South Africa.

speedily to transform themselves into authoritarian one-party systems, usually dominated by a single charismatic leader, standing alone in the spotlight. Nigeria for some years was hailed as the model of the multi-party democratic state in Africa, but its claim to this distinction came to an abrupt end in the 1966 military coups, one of a series of similar events which in a few months changed the political complexion of Africa. In other military overturns, as notably in Ghana, both the one-party state and the charismatic leader, which had come to seem such familiar features on the African political landscape, went into the discard.

The United States, however much Washington may have preferred the more safely conservative regimes, has been catholic in its readiness to work with all kinds of African governments, generally paying only a minimum of attention even to the deliberate provocations of Nkrumah and his associates. Guinea, indeed, despite the radicalism of President Sékou Touré, has been unusually favored among the French-speaking states as far as American aid is concerned, far outclassing its conservative and wealthier neighbor, the Ivory Coast.[8]

In two very different countries, the Congo and Ethiopia, the United States is sometimes charged with having given special backing to a conservative or reactionary regime. Enough has already been said of the Congo to make it unnecessary to recapitulate the story here other than to say that many Africans, in the light particularly of American relations with Lumumba and Tshombe, accused the United States of seeking to circumvent the Congo's liberation in order to ensure capitalist control over a rich country in the heart of Africa.

In the case of Ethiopia, the essential accusation is that the United States has given undue military support—the largest allotted to any African state—to a backward-looking imperial regime, one of whose major bulwarks is an aristocracy of feudal landowners. The issue which is involved came out well in the report to Congress for fiscal 1964 on the Foreign Assistance Program. Bracketing Ethiopia and Libya, this report asserted that military aid helps to ensure continued access to such facilities as the American communications center at Asmara and "also contributes to the internal security of the recipient countries."[9] It is precisely on this latter ground that the new and rising forces in Ethiopia, representing in good part the younger Western-educated elements, object to the form which American aid has taken, since they see the internal security which it provides as furnishing the Emperor and the great landowners

[8] Philippe Decraene calculated that in 1964 American aid to Guinea came to 6 milliards of Guinea francs, while the country's budget was less than 12 milliards. He saw Guinea as unique among African countries, since it survived—thanks to Soviet trade and massive American aid. (*Le Monde*, November 28-29, 1965.) Claire Sterling asserted that nobody in the capital of the Ivory Coast, "growing rich faster than any other new African state," understands why "the United States, generous in aid to the rickety pro-Communist regime in Guinea, should take so little interest in the sturdy anti-Communist state next door—particularly since this is one of the few such states not asking for handouts." ("Houphouet-Biogny Wins a Bet," *The Reporter*, June 16, 1966, p. 29.)

[9] *The Foreign Assistance Program FY 1964*, pp. 33-34.

the police and military means to suppress any movement which aims at modernization.[10]

Even though much of the politically conscious younger generation sees the United States as the main bulwark of a reactionary autocracy, it cannot be ignored that the rest of Africa has given its blessing to the imperial regime by establishing Addis Ababa as a central point for pan-African operations and notably as the headquarters for the OAU and the Economic Commission for Africa. Radical as well as conservative Africa has acknowledged the centrality of Ethiopia despite its geographical remoteness and its anachronistic imperial polity. That Africa should have accepted an Amharic Emperor as one of its major spokesmen in a revolutionary era must be numbered among the more peculiar ironies of our times.

On the face of the record it has been less the United States which has shunned or attacked the radical left-inclined regimes than the latter which have attacked the United States, although many rumors circulate as to CIA activities of all varieties, the truth of which it is usually impossible to determine. Almost anything which happens in the Congo of which left nationalist Africa disapproves is likely to be laid at the door of the CIA; Nkrumah was said to believe that the CIA was out to get him; and Frenchmen resident in Gabon shot at and bombed the American Embassy in Libreville in March, 1964, in the belief that the CIA had incited the revolt against President Mba which was put down by armed French intervention.

For the most part, American diplomatic relations with the African states have gone smoothly; but a few unpleasant incidents have occurred, particularly following American support of Tshombe and the Stanleyville paratroop landing. One unfortunate diplomatic episode involved the expulsion from Tanzania in January, 1965 of two American diplomats, accused of engaging in subversive activities, in what appears to have been a tragi-comedy of error and misunderstanding. Further diplomatic reprisals were promptly taken on both sides. The Tanzanian climate of opinion in which such events took place was illustrated by an editorial in *The Nationalist* of Dar es Salaam, representative of the ruling party, which suggested that the United States should stop throwing its weight around and seeking to buy the good will of poor countries. The condemnation of American policies by all truly independent African states, it held, should persuade Washington to rid itself of the Communist bogey and stop thinking of creating more puppet governments than it already had in the Congo and elsewhere.[11]

An instance in which the United States took strong diplomatic action occurred in August, 1965 when it withdrew its diplomatic and consular

[10] That all is not quite as it should be was acknowledged by AID and the Department of Defense when they informed Congress that Ethiopia's newly-won prominence in Africa could not be maintained unless the country demonstrated leadership and progress in domestic affairs: "United States assistance is designed to support an acceleration of the economic and social development of Ethiopia." (*Proposed Mutual Defense and Development Programs FY 1966*, p. 131.)

[11] *Africa Report*, X, No. 3 (March, 1965), 42. See also *The New York Times*, February 15, 1965.

staffs from Congo-Brazzaville on the grounds that improper treatment of American personnel made it impossible to maintain representation there.[12] President Massemba-Debat denied any hostility to the United States or its people, holding Tshombe's use of American military aid against the interests of Brazzaville largely responsible for the difficulties. "In other countries," he decorously added, "the American Embassy would have been burned to the ground."

A third episode occurred in Burundi when in January, 1966, under peculiar circumstances, the American Ambassador was expelled, upon which Washington asked for the recall of Burundi's Ambassador.

DO THE WINDS OF CHANGE BLOW LEFTWARD?

Second only to the immensely difficult problems posed by white-dominated southern Africa are the dangers for the United States if the next gusts of the winds of change in Africa turn out to be blowing strongly leftward. While this does not appear presently likely, at least a somewhat abstract political logic makes it one of the potentialities in an unstable and unpredictable continent. The genteel transfer of sovereign power to the new countries, the continued close relations with the ex-colonial powers leading to charges of neo-colonialism, and the desire for a speedy swing to socialism and Africanization within a pan-African framework, might all be seen as predisposing toward leftward revolutionary action. The original trio of Guinea, Ghana, and Mali marked out paths which others might follow, and Congo-Brazzaville has moved to the left more recently. Tanzania remains an uncertain quantity, but with evidence of significant leftward pulls. On the other hand, Guinea has in the last years somewhat reversed its course; and, most strikingly of all, the rapid-fire sequence of miltary take-overs starting with Mobutu's coup of November, 1965 in the Congo has contradicted any assumption that the general trend would be to the left. Burundi expelled the Communist Chinese early in 1965 following the assassination of its Premier, and the Central African Republic celebrated New Year's Day, 1966, by a similar move as part of a military coup, followed a day or two later by Dahomey, whose military had seized power in December.

The applicability to Africa of the terms "left" and "right," or "radical" and "conservative," carrying with them so many European connotations, may very properly be questioned. In particular they are dubious terms when applied to the new military regimes. The pattern is a confusing one: the military are unlikely to be seriously leftist in orientation, but they can also not automatically be assumed to be conservative or reactionary. If Ghana's new government is to the right of that of Nkrumah, the same cannot be said of the Congo where General Mobutu is not to be placed to the right of Tshombe, nor can the military governments of Nigeria be automatically assumed to be more conservative than the civilian regime which was overthrown.

In a rough fashion, however, a leftward or radical inclination may be

---

[12] *Department of State Bulletin,* LIII, No. 1366 (August 30, 1965); *Africa Report,* X, No. 9 (October, 1965), 42.

seen where the emphasis is on speedy Africanization, socialism, pan-Africanism, and a neutralism benevolent to Moscow or Peking, with a corresponding cooling of relations with the West. Virtually by definition such a leftward swing may be assumed to be hostile to the United States which is pilloried by all good leftists as the leader of the imperialists.[13] Precisely those factors which eased the American relationship with most of the new African states could make relations very difficult in revolutionary circumstances. The United States is in greater or less degree committed to the existing regimes while opposition forces tend to attract the backing of the Communists. Washington must view with almost as much disfavor as do the African governments the claim of Chou En-lai that Africa is ripe for revolution—although the revolutions, or approximations thereof, which have taken place of late have generally headed toward the middle of the road rather than to the left.

All this is far from implying that the United States has a clear and open road ahead of it in Africa. The catalog of pitfalls and roadblocks is a familiar one. As far back as 1956 Tom Mboya of Kenya wrote of a growing sense of "puzzled disappointment" as Africans measured the actual policies of the United States against its reputation as the symbol of the anti-colonial struggle.[14] Since then, the cautious approach of the United States to the issues of greatest concern to the Africans has contrasted sharply with the vigor and immediacy of its response to anything seen as a Communist threat. In a television interview shown on January 2, 1966, President Nyerere classified the United States as the leading imperialist power because it was the leader among the Western states which had imposed colonial rule on Africa; and Secretary-General U Thant of the UN saw the American people as worried by political and social changes elsewhere:

> The revolt of the colonial peoples, who are in fact the ultimate heirs of 1776, and their desire to fashion their own way of life, seems to be rather frightening and incomprehensible to the descendants of those who started it all at Lexington and Concord.[15]

The United States is revolutionary in its example and in the social and economic development which it stimulates, but its present tendency is to be conservative in its political attitudes and actions. Examples of the diffi-

[13] "The great majority of left-wing radicals in the world—including American radicals—have in their temperament an inherent anti-American bias. There is a sense in which it is almost a logical contradiction to be left-wing and pro-American at the same time. . . . It can almost be said that the colonial situation had suppressed a latent anti-Americanism in African radical thought. . . . But once colonialism retreated it was inevitable that sooner or later radicalism in Africa should take the same anti-Yankee turn that it had taken elsewhere." (Ali A. Mazrui, "African Diplomatic Thought and the Principle of Legitimacy," in *The Congo, Africa and America*, ed. Gary Gappert and Garry Thomas. Occasional Paper No. 15. Syracuse, New York: Maxwell Graduate School of Citizenship and Public Affairs, Syracuse University, 1965.)

[14] Tom Mboya, "Our Revolutionary Tradition: An African View," *Current History*, December, 1956, p. 345.

[15] *United Nations Review*, X, No. 1 (January, 1963), 58.

culties and dilemmas, the opportunities and dangers which confront the United States in Africa can be found at every turning. Always in the background or foreground stands the issue of racial discrimination at home: Harlem and Watts, Little Rock and Selma have achieved an international notoriety and are fair game for anyone who wants to exploit them.

The economic influence of the United States, the most affluent of affluent societies, is penetrating everywhere more and more insistently. American military and political power are immense, and the United States has shown no marked reluctance to use them beyond its borders. What are the prospects, Africans inevitably ask, that it will apply them in Africa, and that the Congo or some other territory will become another Korea or Vietnam? In the simplest terms, Africans fear that the United States will push them around, intentionally or inadvertently, no doubt protesting that it is all for their own good and in the service of the anti-Communist cause.

A peculiarly puzzling difficulty concerns the furnishing of military equipment and training for African states. It is tragic folly that poor countries must spend their own substance and foreign aid on building up military forces beyond the needs of domestic security. Aside from their possible employment in intra-African police actions, the only likely external use of such forces is in warfare with neighboring states which it is surely in neither the general nor the American interest to promote. Yet if the United States refuses to assist in building up African armed forces, other countries will no doubt gladly accept the responsibility, particularly if it is a plausible assumption that such forces are likely to be a country's next rulers. Furthermore, strengthening one country's military forces inevitably causes disaffection among its less favored neighbors, as in the case of Somalia's displeasure at the American arming of Ethiopia. Is it conceivable that with Africa's full consent, some scheme for the international limitation of African arms and perhaps of neutralization of the continent might be worked out? [16]

For the United States openly to espouse some African cause is almost inevitably to prejudice against it many Africans who will seek out such sinister motives as they can discover. To mention only a single example, although the United States is accused of working on the time-honored principle of "divide and rule," it has in fact been inclined to promote both regionalism and at least a loose form of continent-wide pan-Africanism, plus such functional collaboration as can be achieved. The widening of the economic base for development, including industrialization, seems essential for all African states, even though the wealthier among them, such as the Ivory Coast and Gabon, like Tshombe's Katanga, have shown little inclination to share their relative prosperity. Another fertile field for action is the multistate development of river basins, for which several projects are under way, as, for example, for the Niger in which eight African states are engaged. It is in keeping with American policy to do

[16] See Arnold Rivkin, *Africa and the West: Elements of Free-World Policy.* (Center for International Studies, Massachusetts Institute of Technology. New York: Praeger, 1962, p. 62.) The UN General Assembly gave its blessing in December, 1965, to a declaration on the denuclearization of Africa.

. what it can, through AID and otherwise, to encourage African states to seek out the broader horizons which the continent offers, but American spokesmen would do well to temper any overt enthusiasm for particular programs or enterprises.

If the economic advantages are the most obvious, it is also evident that an effectively organized Africa would be politically advantageous on various scores. The availability of African machineries to assist in the settlement of disputes would have great utility, as already demonstrated in the success of the OAU in putting an end to the fighting between Morocco and Algeria and between Somalia and Ethiopia. To look optimistically into a future not presently visible, it would be helpful if African forces, coordinated by regional or pan-African bodies, were available to undertake the policing of such troubled areas as might necessitate outside intervention, as, perhaps, following the liberation of Portuguese territories from colonial rule.

SOUTHERN AFRICA

The grimmest tragedy which could befall Africa and all countries concerned with it would be a state of warfare between independent Black Africa and white-dominated southern Africa across the Zambesi. At its by no means inconceivable worst this could become an African race war into which other peoples might be drawn on a global basis, even furnishing the setting for World War III. Unless drastic and unexpected changes revolutionize the political and social systems of southern Africa, it must be assumed that African insistence on the overthrow of white supremacy will constantly grow. Such insistence can count on the support of much of Asia, the Communists, and a broad sweep of left-liberal opinion throughout the world, although it is impossible to predict what countries would take what kind of action beyond diplomatic pronouncements and UN speeches. The United States and Britain, hesitant to join even in strongly worded UN resolutions, have left no doubt of their far greater reluctance to join in sanctions or such military action as might be required to enforce a blockade or overthrow a government. To a greater extent than African countries, they are likely to be restrained, among other considerations, by awareness of the grievous results which could flow from the enforcement of sanctions against South Africa and her neighbors. Leaving aside the question as to how much damage and suffering sanctions would inflict on Africans in the country—a matter which African leaders have consistently held to be not a relevant consideration—it is a wide open gamble what manner of governments and societies might emerge in southern African countries if their economies were ruined and their present regimes overthrown by force.

In circumstances such as these it becomes necessary to contemplate the possibility of a fundamental withdrawal of African confidence from the United States and Britain, accompanied by a deliberate turn to the USSR or China, or both, as the powers on which Africa would rely for full backing. Southern Africa thus promises to become—perhaps it has already become—the crucible in which Africans will test the good faith of the

West in paying more than lip service to the cause of African emancipation. The failure to take stronger action against Ian Smith's rebel government in Rhodesia has already seriously eroded African confidence in the West.

In his first major speech on African affairs, delivered on May 26, 1966 to a gathering of African ambassadors in Washington on the third anniversary of the OAU, President Johnson reaffirmed the traditional American position that governments must derive their just powers from the consent of the governed and asserted this to be the core of political freedom and the first principle of nation-building.[17] Citing the American experience, he assured the ambassadors that the United States is, heart and soul, with the African countries in their effort to rid themselves of the waste and injustice resulting from the domination of one race by another. He found that across the African continent

> the majority of people prefer self-government with peril to subservience with serenity. [A peculiar word to use in the circumstances.] This makes all the more repugnant the narrow and outmoded policy which in some parts of Africa permits the few to rule at the expense of the many.

These are brave words, reiterating the stand which the United States has regularly taken at least since Sharpeville; but the words must be measured against the fact that the United States, officially and privately, has maintained substantially full intercourse with South Africa, and a number of Americans have profited handsomely from their South African connections, as testimony before the House Subcommittee on Africa investigating United States-South African relations early in 1966 brought out in detail.[18] With the exception of the arms embargo, the United States had by the beginning of 1967 taken virtually no steps to move toward the policy of disengagement from South Africa in all spheres elaborated by George M. Houser, Executive Director of the American Committee on Africa, in his testimony before this subcommittee. Diplomatic relations continued in full force and the tracking stations were maintained, with a *de facto* acceptance in both instances of the South African ban on non-white personnel. Trade and investment continued at relatively high levels, and the American quota for South African sugar had recently been increased.

It would be folly to pretend that there are any simple and pleasant answers or to think that the United States is likely to be able to escape highly painful decisions. As Assistant Secretary of State Williams informed the House Subcommittee on the opening day of its hearings, "we must frankly admit that the problems that we and other like-minded nations face regarding South Africa remain virtually intractable." Hope should not be abandoned that goals which both Africans and Americans desire can be achieved by non-violent means, but if non-violence proves

[17] *The New York Times*, May 27, 1966.
[18] *United States-South African Relations, Hearings.* For the testimony of George M. Houser, referred to in the next sentence, see pp. 190-211. His recommendations were summarized in *Africa Today*, March, 1966.

as ineffective as Africans usually assume, then the dangers inevitably accompanying mandatory sanctions and the use of force must be weighed against the losses involved in a breach with the forces which seek majoritarian solutions in keeping with the temper of the times. On the latter score, Hugh Foot, now Lord Caradon and Britain's Ambassador to the UN, has stated the matter well, asserting his belief that:

> Before long the United States, leaving aside considerations of profit, will come to the conclusion that it simply cannot face the prospect of a color war starting in South Africa—with Soviet Russia and Red China and all the new nations of Africa and Asia on the winning side but with the United States backing the losing forces of white domination.[19]

The simplest realism demands recognition that the way in which the black African states have conducted their affairs since independence can inspire no abundant confidence that southern Africa, liberated from white domination, will develop stable democratic governments which promote development. The record of the newly independent states north of the Zambesi, and of the older ones as well for that matter, is a very mixed one. The Nigerian time of troubles culminating in the assassinations and murderous feuds associated with the two military coups of January and August, 1966, made all the more bitter by Nigeria's reputation for stability and democracy, was a striking demonstration of the precarious foundations upon which all African polities rest. The transition of Africa from colonialism to independence and from its traditional communities to modernity will be a stormy one.

Two major difficulties confront those who shape American policy toward Africa: racial discrimination at home, which Secretary of State Rusk characterized as "The biggest single burden that we carry on our backs in our foreign relations in the 1960's," and the lack of any widespread, coherent, and broadly based body of opinion which is seriously concerned with Africa. The issue of racial discrimination, which gravely affects the credibility of our expressions of good will for Africans, is being directly attacked by the massive, but still only spottily successful, drive for equality and desegregation—a drive which, as has been seen, has its intimate relations to the overthrow of colonialism and the rise of the new Africa. The same drive seems certain also to strengthen significantly the ranks of those concerned with Africa. As Negro Americans achieve better education and larger prosperity, their interest in Africa will grow, and their effective enfranchisement will give them the political power which they have hitherto lacked. Together with the growing body of other

---

[19] Hugh Foot, "The Whites in Africa," *Saturday Review*, July 25, 1964. p. 12. Martin Luther King has excoriated the present American policy as constituting "massive support" of South Africa: "The shame of our nation is that it is objectively an ally of this monstrous government in its grim war with its own black people." (*Africa Today*, December, 1965, p. 10.)

Americans who are in one way or another involved in African affairs, they will both press for a more vigorous American policy and rouse and inform American public opinion.

It is impossible to evade the presumption that in the coming years the United States and the world at large will be confronted in Africa with more coups and upheavals, more violence and revolutions, than have been seen up to now. In consequence, the choices which the United States will have to make, not only in southern Africa but in the length and breadth of the continent, are likely to be tougher than those which it has faced so far, although the Congo and Rhodesia and the spread of assassinations and military regimes have foreshadowed the problems which lie ahead. If the American policy toward Africa is to be one of studied moderation, fearful of change and laying its stress on stability, the United States may well find itself increasingly out of touch with the rising new forces. It is evident both that revolutions have many dangers and that left-leaning elements are prone to be instinctively hostile to the United States, but stability which leads to stagnation can be no answer. Even in a short long-run, the risks of seeking to come to terms with the progressive forces are less than those flowing from being inextricably bound to an old order whose life draws toward an end.

In the first decade of decolonization following Ghana's independence, Africa was to a surprising degree spared the major boundary disputes and attempts by one state to conquer its neighbor, which have so often characterized international intercourse elsewhere. The boundaries laid down by the colonial powers, defining the states which now divide most of the continent between them, have been accepted by almost all the governments, and attacks upon these boundaries have been regarded as challenging the foundations of the African political system. If the precedents of the rest of the world apply, it is all too probable that the fallings-out among African states will take more violent forms in the future than they have hitherto, despite the regard which all profess to have for pan-Africanism. What would be the effect on its neighbors and other parts of Africa if a large state such as Nigeria or the Congo were to disintegrate into its component ethnic parts, perhaps tempting others to intervene for their own prestige or profit? With the open demonstration of the ability of even small armed forces to overturn governments, how serious is the risk that political or military leaders will move beyond the domestic to the external scene and seek to extend their domain by force? Assuming that such things come to pass, the United States will have to make up its mind as to the role it should play. No sensible answer is possible without a knowledge of the particular circumstances of concrete incidents, but as a general proposition it seems clear that the United States would be well advised to aid in the search for peaceful solutions through such international agencies as the OAU and the UN. Unilateral intervention and, worst of all, military intervention by the United States would involve the danger of stirring up more and worse trouble than it could cure.

Wherever possible, as it should be for most purposes, the United States must deal with African countries and problems in their own right, not allowing either European alliances or Cold War considerations to distort the direct relationship. Inevitably reserving the right to differ, the United States and the countries of Africa should continuously seek out the highest levels of agreement and collaboration which they can attain. With full recognition that it promises to be a long and difficult haul, it appears on all scores clearly to be in the American interest to see Africa successfully achieve social and economic development and move ahead toward political strength and unity. Without either assuming the role of God or acting as a global policeman, the United States is in a position to make outstanding contributions to Africa's advancement, and African friendship can be of great moment to the United States.

Bibliography

Brzezinski, Zbigniew, ed., *Africa and the Communist World*. Stanford, Calif.: Stanford University, 1963.

Clendenen, Clarence C. and Peter Duignan, *The United States and the African Slave Trade, 1619-1862*. Hoover Institution Studies. Stanford, Calif.: Stanford University, 1963.

_____, *Americans in Black Africa up to 1865*. Hoover Institution Studies. Stanford, Calif.: Stanford University, 1964.

Clendenen, Clarence C., Robert Collins, and Peter Duignan, *Americans in Africa, 1865-1900*. Hoover Institution Studies. Stanford, Calif.: Stanford University, 1966.

Coleman, James S. and Carl G. Rosberg, eds., *Political Parties and National Integration in Tropical Africa*. Los Angeles and Berkeley: University of California, 1964.

Emerson, Rupert and Martin Kilson, eds., *The Political Awakening of Africa*. Englewood Cliffs, N.J.: Prentice-Hall, 1965. A Spectrum Book.

Goldschmidt, Walter, ed., *The United States and Africa*, rev. ed. New York: Praeger, 1963.

Hance, William A., *The Geography of Modern Africa*. New York and London: Columbia University, 1964.

Hargreaves, John D., *Prelude to the Partition of West Africa*. London: Macmillan, 1963.

Legum, Colin, *Pan-Africanism*, rev. ed. New York: Praeger, 1965.

Lewis, W. Arthur, *Politics in West Africa*. London: G. Allen, 1965.

McKay, Vernon, *Africa in World Politics*. New York: Harper, 1963.

Nielsen, Waldemar A., *African Battleline*. New York: Harper, 1965.

Oliver, Roland and John D. Fage, *A Short History of Africa*. Baltimore: Penguin, 1962.

Padelford, Norman J. and Rupert Emerson, *Africa and World Order*. New York: Praeger, 1963.

Robinson, Ronald and John Gallagher with Alice Denny, *Africa and the Victorians*. London: Macmillan, 1961.

Rotberg, Robert I., *A Political History of Tropical Africa*. New York: Harcourt, 1965.

Wallerstein, Immanuel, *Africa: The Politics of Independence*. New York: Vintage, 1961.

Index

A

Aborigines Rights Protection Society, 3
Adebo, S. O., 57
Adoula, Cyrille, 65
African-American Institute, 48
African Education Commissions, 45
Afro-American relations, summary:
    1865-1945, 15-20
    1945-1955, 21-24
    1955-1961, 24-28
Agricultural production, 11-12
Aid programs, U.S.:
    Africa, 26-27, 35-39
    the Congo, 31, 37, 39-40, 48, 66-67,
      69-70, 101
    Ethiopia, 36, 37, 46
    Ghana, 40
    Guinea, 40, 101
    Liberia, 36, 40
    Nigeria, 39
    South Africa, 40
    (*see also* Military aid)
Algeria, 4
Angola, 9, 31, 50, 70, 71, 72-76
Anticommunism, and U.S. policy, 97,
    100, 104
Apartheid, 61, 84-86
ASPAU (African Scholarship Program
    of American Universities), 47
Awolowo, Obafemi, 20n

Azikiwe, Nnamdi (Zik), 20, 46
Azores, U.S. military base, 70, 75

B

Baldwin, James, 53
Basutoland, 61
Bayard, Thomas F., 16
Bechuanaland, 61
Berlin Conference of 1884-1885, 16
Boer War, 16
Botswana, 61, 89
Bowles, Chester, 23
Brazzaville Conference, 19
Britain:
    and decolonization, 3-4, 19
    and Rhodesia, 79
    and South Africa, 88-89
British West Africa, 20
Bureau of African Affairs, 25
Burundi, 103
Byroade, Henry A., 5

C

Catholic missions, 49-50
Central African Republic, 14, 103
Central Intelligence Agency, 63, 66n,
    102

I

Imperialism, 98
Income, per capita, 11
Independence, *see* Decolonization
Investment, U.S., in Africa, 33-35
Isaacs, Harold R., 55
Islam, 51
Ivory Coast, 11, 12, 13, 101

J

Jeune Afrique poll, 96n
Johnson, Lyndon B., 38, 39, 67, 81, 95, 107
Jurisdiction, UN:
    Portuguese colonies, 71-72, 74-75
    Rhodesia, 79-80

K

Kamarck, Andrew M., 12, 31-32, 42n
Kasavubu, Joseph, 66, 69
Katanga, 62-63, 65-66
Kennedy, John F., 1, 4, 24, 25, 27-28, 36, 45, 65, 95
Kenya, 4, 9, 11, 14, 78
Kiewiet, C.W. de, 93
King, Martin Luther, 108n
Kitawala movement, 51
Korry, Edward M., 38

L

Languages of Africa, 9-10
League of Nations, 17, 18
"Leftist" states, 60, 103-4
Leopold, King of Belgium, 62
Lesotho, 61, 89
Liberia:
    history, 16, 17-18
    strategic use, 17-18, 31
    U.S. aid, 36, 40
    U.S. investment, 34
Libya, 31, 36, 40
Louw, Eric, 90
Lumumba, Patrice, 1, 65, 67

M

Macmillan, Harold, 90
Madagascar, 4, 31
Malawi, 14, 61 (*see also* Nyasaland)
Mali, 11, 13, 60
Mandate system, 16-17

Maryland restaurants, 56
Mau Mau, 4
Mazrui, Ali A., 104n
Mba, Leon, 98, 102
Mboya, Tom, 104
McGhee, George, 22
McKay, Vernon, 5n, 24, 25
Militant "progressive" states, 60, 103-4
Military aid:
    to the Congo, 66-69
    to Portugal, 74-75
    risks, 105
    to South Africa, 91
    U.S. programs, 37
Military coups, 13-14
Missionaries, 49-51
Mobutu, Joseph, 69
Morocco, 16, 31, 36, 37
Mozambique, 9, 70, 76, 82
Mussolini, Benito, 17, 18

N

National Council of the Churches of Christ, 50-51
Nationalism, 3, 20, 95-97
NATO, 72, 73, 75, 100
Négritude, 9
Negro Americans, and Africa, 16, 20, 25-26, 52-58
Neo-colonialism, 2, 35, 36
Neutralism, African, 6-7
Nielsen, Waldemar A., 85n, 93n
Nigeria:
    and the Congo, 2, 69
    independence, 3, 20, 24
    missionaries, 49
    Peace Corps, 43
    politics, 13, 14, 35, 61, 97
    population, 9
    strategic importance, 31, 32
    University, 46
    U.S. aid, 39
Nixon, Richard, 7, 26
Nkrumah, Kwame, 4, 12, 24, 40, 44, 73, 80n, 97, 101, 154
Norstad, Lauris, 87
Northern Rhodesia, 48, 61, 78, 82
Nyasaland, 4, 51, 78 (*see also* Federation of Rhodesia and Nyasaland, Malawi)
Nyerere, Julius, 13, 84, 97, 104

O

OAU (Organization of African Unity), 2, 69, 76, 82, 102, 106

DATE DUE